CONTENTS

WELCOME

Rt Rev Dr Derek Browning

Moderator of the General Assembly of the Church of Scotland

How should we include children and young people in our Church's life and worship? The Church has swung over the years from treating children like little adults, without reference to their needs or abilities, to infantilising worship through 'family services' which can often lack imagination or intellectual stimulation for either child or adult. Some of the dirge-like 'children's hymns' of yesteryear have at least been rivalled by and probably eclipsed by some of the dreary ditties of some contemporary composers who think endless repetition of performance-focused 'praise items' is a substitute for well written, theologically literate, congregation-including hymns and songs. The danger always seems to lie in trying to create a 'one-size-fits-all' response which usually leaves everyone feeling frustrated, unnoticed, or, worst of all, ignored.

This new production from the Learn series will not answer every question, nor indeed will it meet with universal welcome. That is good! What it will do is enable and encourage thoughtful and informed discussion in this important area of our Church's life. The aim will not be to produce a blueprint of what to do, but rather a launch pad for what might be considered within the context of different congregations. It will give examples from experience, and will challenge us to consider again how we include all God's children, whatever their age, within the life and worship of our Church.

I was recently challenged by a former politician to see if there was something we could do to reclaim the word 'family' as a concept and a reality within our society, and within the Church. Family is no longer solely made up of two parents with their two-point-four children. We live in a time when the reality of the 'nuclear family' is being reframed as much as what used to be called the 'extended family'. 'Family' should be a broad church encompassing young and old, married and single and all the other nuances of contemporary human culture. Churches, among their many unique selling points, provide opportunities for people from different generations to gather together in general or more specific groups, to explore, wonder, learn and worship. The economy of God in worship is flexible enough to be a broad economy, with many strands and layers and textures in both Word and Sacraments.

I hope this book will not give you all the answers you need, but will help you find the questions. ∎

BEING CHURCH TOGETHER

CHILDREN AND YOUNG PEOPLE IN THE BIBLE

Grant Barclay
Minister of Orchardhill Parish Church

L ife in Old and New Testament time, was quite different from ours. Even so, Biblical principles of protecting children and young people, nurturing them, and expecting that they will play a full part in faith communities remain relevant and are a reminder that all ages belong together in vibrant worshipping, serving and flourishing churches.

In the Old Testament

Faith was a family activity in Old Testament times. Children were to be taught Israel's history (Deuteronomy 4.9) and God's law (Deuteronomy 6.7) so that, knowing their heritage, they might live faithfully obedient lives (1 Kings 8.25). The Passover liturgy, worship that took place within a family setting, required children to ask what the meal means in a celebration that identified all those present as the people whom God had freed from captivity (Exodus 12.26, 13.14).

This emphasis both on nurture for faithful adult life and present membership of a faith community means young people are seen neither as property to be exploited, nor only as potential future contributors. Children themselves are seen to be inherently valuable, a divine blessing (Proverbs 17.6). Abusive treatment of children, such as other nations' practice of making children 'pass through fire' (perhaps a form of child sacrifice, as mentioned in Ezekiel 20.25, Jeremiah 19.5) is consistently condemned. God's people have a duty to safeguard the vulnerable, and this always includes children.

However, as members of God's people, children and young people have responsibilities. The fifth commandment demands they honour their parents (Exodus 20.12). Children are involved not only in learning, but also in practising, their faith. As children have early, and continuing, active involvement with God's people, so they grow. Amos points to children being raised to become prophets (Amos 2.11), with no suggestion they will only prophesy as adults. Joel's description, endorsed at Pentecost, has 'young men' seeing visions from God, with daughters and sons prophesying (Joel 2.28). Prophets anticipate that young people, as the norm and not the exception will bear God's message to God's whole people. Samuel hears and serves God (unlike the aged Eli) when he is still young (1 Samuel 3) and continues that faithful service throughout his life.

Children's full and broad participation is underlined in Zechariah 8, an idealised vision of a renewed Jerusalem where people of great age sit safely in their doorways while children play in the street. The Hebrew words used suggest this all happens in the city's commercial and civic centre, not in some forgotten back alley. Children, young people, and all ages belong together in God's purposes.

In the New Testement

This vision of participation runs through the New Testament. There, children are found among early groups of Jesus-followers. These include household units that, if Timothy's example is typical, consciously develop children's faith (2 Timothy 3.15). Such nurture, combined with a call to children to be obedient, is found in the repetition and development of the fifth commandment in Ephesians 6.1-4 and Colossians 3.20-21, which is now expanded to include paternal responsibility. An almost passing snapshot of the early church in Tyre includes children and wives among the church members who wave Paul off (Acts 21.5). Children are nurtured in faith and are not excluded from significant, even emotional, events in the fellowship's life.

The Gospels offer extended reflection on Jesus' teaching and practice and are a highpoint of Christian understanding of the place of younger generations in the Church. The young Jesus shows by example that religious institutions are proper places for young people to grow by searching, and questioning – and being welcomed – as he calls the Temple his 'Father's house', engaging with scholars and priests, and being encouraged to do so (Luke 2.49).

In his adult ministry, Jesus reserves severe condemnation for those who cause 'little ones to stumble' (Luke 17.2), reminding us of an ongoing duty to safeguard all those who are vulnerable. He criticises those who keep parents from bringing their children - by no means only babies - to him, for blessing (Matthew 19.13); and he places a child literally centre stage among his disciples as an illustration of what it means to 'receive' the kingdom of God' (Mark 10.15). Jesus does not advocate childishness but compels a radical re-imagining both of God's kingdom and the place of children and young people within Christian faith communities.

For today

The world has changed much since these texts were written, but key principles endure. There is an absolute duty to protect and safeguard. There is the obligation of older generations to nurture those who are young to enable them to flourish now and in the future as committed disciples, something that goes far beyond entertaining, or amusing, and certainly precludes marginalising them.

Quite the reverse: churches should enable children and young people to hear God's call to them to recognise their valued place in God's care for all, and to respond to God by playing their full part as young members of Christ's body. This participation is itself valuable: young people help us understand how to perceive God's kingdom; their absence from Christian fellowships impoverishes all. Such involvement also enables them to mature into adult disciples with different, and no less valuable, contributions to make towards God's purposes for the world and the Church.

In the Bible we read of God's call to the whole Christian community to affirm God's image in children, to recognise their place within Christian fellowships and to enable them to flourish through active engagement with all generations. Only by being people of all ages together will we flourish fully as Christ's church. ∎

THINK

What difference does it make to your thinking that young people are not only to be nurtured, but have important parts to play within church while they are young? What might some of these roles be?

How do we make church a proper place for children and young people to learn, explore, question and grow – and to be welcomed as they do all this?

In what ways do we expect to hear God's message for the church today through the voices of those who are young?

Do we see church as impoverished if any age-groups or generations are missing? What challenges might younger generations make to long held views and ways of worshipping and working?

READ

Anne Richards, **Children in the Bible: a fresh approach,** (London: SPCK publishing, 2013)

Marcia J. Bunge (ed.), **The Child in the Bible,** (Grand Rapids: Wm. B Eerdmans Publishing, 2008)

ACT

Challenge your team and or your Kirk Session to create a list of all the times the Bible talks about children and young people. Encourage each meeting to begin by exploring one of them further.

Consider exploring these passages and stories with children and young people. Is their experience of childhood the same or different? Why might that be?

RESOURCE

The Scottish Bible Society
www.scottishbiblesociety.org/

Youth and Children's Work magazine
www.youthandchildrens.work

CHILDREN AND YOUNG PEOPLE IN THE CHURCH

Suzi Farrant

Young People and Young Adult's Development Worker,
Mission and Discipleship Council

Each of us, perhaps based on our own experience, has a different idea as to the place of children and young people in the Church.

Sunday schools are an integral part of the lives of most congregations; in fact those congregations that are unable to sustain one due to lack of leaders or lack of children often perceive themselves as failing. But is this the best way of being church and passing on the faith to the next generation? Even the name can conjure up images of endless colouring in, prayer drills and being told what Bible stories mean, rather than images of children encountering God and joining adults on the journey of faith. If the Church is to be a gathering of the whole people of God for worship how do children and young people fit into that?

My experience

I grew up in the Church, so Sunday school was a regular part of my week; it was the thing that you always knew was coming and offered structure in the complex world of growing up. As a young child there were quite a number of others around my age and we loved to play together, particularly getting in the way during coffee time as we chased each other around the building letting off all our pent-up energy having spent perhaps too much time sitting at a table doing a craft.

I have many happy memories of being involved in that congregation as a child and will be forever grateful to all those there who played a part in my faith journey. But as I look back there are also things I would question. One moment that sticks in my memory is of my brother's and cousin's dedication service when I was six years old. My parents had chosen my favourite song to be sung as part of the service but the minister had scheduled it for after the children would have left the service to go to Sunday school. As I recall it, I kicked up a bit of a fuss, not understanding why it couldn't be before I left, or indeed why I had to leave at all as this was clearly to be a special family service and being part of the family I thought I should be there. In the end a compromise was reached and I was allowed to stay in the service after all the other children had left so I could sing the song and then I left joining the Sunday school some 5-10 minutes after everyone else - a seemingly small incident, but nearly thirty years later I can still remember it so it obviously made a big impression on me.

As a teenager, the number of my peers within the church had somewhat reduced although there were still enough to make having a youth group viable. Now though, those from my generation are all but lost to that congregation - some of us have moved on to other congregations as our lives have moved us out of the area, but there remains a significant proportion that are no longer connected to the Church. This picture is also repeated elsewhere.

Recent research

Recent statistics about young people and the church are telling. According to the Sticky Faith research undertaken by the Fuller Youth Institute, 50% of youth group graduates struggle significantly with faith once they've left school and end up leaving the church, and six in every seven young people report feeling underprepared for a life of faith outside their youth group. Clearly the things we are doing, even though they may look great for a time, are not working in the long term.

The Faith in Our Families research report[1] from Care for the Family shows just how important the family is in nurturing faith and argues that as churches we need to do more to support parents and guardians as they raise their children. I wonder if the Sunday school model, which has seen the church family delegating the responsibility of passing on the faith to Sunday school teachers, has played a part in the deskilling of parents and other family members for their role in the task.

Sharing the journey of faith

Despite our best intentions, I think we've fallen into the trap of viewing children as empty vessels to be filled with knowledge about the faith rather than fellow pilgrims on a journey of faith, and so we've borrowed educational methods from schools and created a curriculum, segregating according to age. Our Sunday morning services are for our children and young people less about worship and encountering God and more about learning; our services are generally structured in such a way that children are only present for the first couple of hymns/songs, a prayer and a children's talk before being ushered out to their own activities, while young people are not present in worship at all being in their own activities the whole time. No matter how good these activities are (and in lots of cases, although not all, they are brilliant), to me operating in this way means we are all missing out: children are missing out on part of the richness and diversity of the Church and an encounter with God through participation in worship, and the Church is missing out on the joy, exuberance and questioning spirit of children.

I am in no doubt that we need to learn about our faith, and a really important part of that is through age specific/targeted groups; I'm just not convinced that these groups should take the place of worship services or indeed just be for children and young people. What would it look like to have all ages worshipping together on a Sunday morning and then at some other point during the week to have for all ages a group for the purpose of learning, segregated according to age or shared interests or stages of faith development? Could it be a community of faith with everyone seen as a fellow pilgrim regardless of their age and experience? ∎

1. Faith in our families: a research report, https://www.careforthefamily.org.uk/wp-content/uploads/2017/03/Faith-in-our-Families-Research-booklet.pdf [accessed 9th June 2017]

THINK

Did God envisage the Church to be segregated by age?

What is your experience of Sunday school? What are the advantages and disadvantages of Sunday schools as a model?

What helps your own faith to develop? Are there ways children and young people can be involved and join you on that journey?

READ

John H. Westerhoff III, **Will Our Children Have Faith?,** (New York: Morehouse Publishing, 3rd Revised Edition, 2012)

Ivy Beckwith and David M. Csinos, **Children's Ministry in the Way of Jesus,** (Illinois: IVP, 2013)

Kara E. Powell, Brad M. Griffin, and Cheryl Crawford, **Sticky Faith Youth Worker Edition: practical ideas to nurture long-term faith in teenagers,** (Grand Rapids: Zondervan, 2011)

David M. Csinos, **Children's Ministry That Fits: beyond one size fits all approaches to nurturing children's spirituality,** (Oregon: Wipf & Stock, 2011)

ACT

Consider the balance of learning and worship that your children and young people are involved in each week. Are there ways you can change that balance?

Use the Godly Play method of exploring a bible story to wonder together at what God is saying to you through the passage.

Host a prayer space in the church for all ages, encouraging families to use it to pray together.

RESOURCE

Jerome W. Berryman, **Teaching Godly Play: how to mentor the spiritual development of children**, (Denver: Moorhouse Education Resources, 2009)

Carrie Kingston and Isobel MacDougall, **Children in the Way? Creative opportunities for churches with young children**, (Oxford: Monarch Books, 2011)

Martin Saunders, **The Beautiful Disciplines: helping young people to develop their spiritual roots**, (Oxford: Monarch Books, 2011)

INTERGENERATIONAL CHURCH

Gareth Crispin

PhD student, Cliff College, Calver, UK

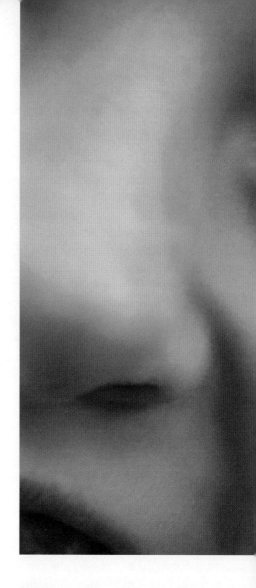

Sometimes it's audible isn't it? The collective sigh of relief when the minister says, "And now the children and young people will leave for their groups". It means ministers can get on with the 'real business' in hand, parents can relax, and children and young people can go to age specific groups aimed at catering for their specific needs.

In an age when many congregations have no children and young people in Sunday services, their mere presence in the wider church community is to be celebrated, but are we missing out on the blessings that might come from closer interaction between people of different generations?

Interaction and mutuality

Interaction lies at the heart of intergenerational church, an idea that has received growing attention in the last few years. It is not simply multi-generational, with people of different generations in the same location, even in the same all age service. No, intergenerational church is specifically all about actual, meaningful interaction between people of different generations and so also is more about the whole life of the church community rather than simply the Sunday services. In short, it's about what it means to live as a Christian community.

As well as interaction, mutuality is central to intergenerational church. Children and young people are full members of the church and so are not to be patronised or ignored. They are to interact with others as equals with something to contribute. Their different perspective may provide the catalyst for others to remember the awe that God should inspire or the sheer joy of understanding the Father's love for us, or the simple trust that Jesus invites us to place in him. Equally, they may ask difficult questions that others have long since buried as they have 'matured' in faith.

This doesn't commit us to a church that then ignores or patronises older generations, a risk in our contemporary society with its idolatry of the new. Instead, true mutuality recognises that older generations bring

> ❝ **But why are we talking about this now? Why not 50 years ago?**

continuity and wisdom, knowledge of the story of our faith and a witness to God's grace in their lives over many years.

The Bible

Equally, intergenerational church doesn't commit us to a church, focused only on the views and experiences of people, without Biblical authority and teaching. Mutuality doesn't imply that whatever anyone says is to be accepted and left uncontested. However, it does mean church leaders fostering new ways of discipleship, including the development of new skills of pastoral oversight to gently shepherd God's people as they interact on a mutual footing.

Of course you, can't find a proof text in the bible that says: "thou shalt never segregate along age lines" but examples of the community of faith being taught together should at least give us pause for thought (e.g. Deuteronomy 6, Exodus 16.9-10 and 35.1-4; Ephesians 6.1-3) while Ephesians chapter 4 should give us even more to ponder: Paul reminds the church in Ephesus that as Christians they are all bound together to the one body through the one Lord (Ephesians 4.4-5). In this context Paul implores them to bear with one another in love (Ephesians 4.2), which is difficult if interaction is non-existent![2]

Adoption in Christ means old and young are brothers and sisters in Christ; maybe viewing others in the church more like this may help in our intergenerational relationships.

For today

But why are we talking about this now? Why not fifty years ago? Well, of course, people have always talked about it, but it has come increasingly onto the agenda in the last couple of decades for a variety of reasons.

It is likely that part of the catalyst for change has come from the feeling that the segmented models of children and youth ministry that have developed since the late nineteenth century have not turned the tide of falling numbers. Those models, developed in the context

2. Here Paul assumes children are present at the reading of his letter to the church.

of modern industrial societies with a focus on management and efficiency, reflected the wider segmentation within society as seen within the establishment of the state schooling system.

The last few decades have seen some questioning of these foundational ideals of the nineteenth century, including seeking new forms of community and a sense of the importance of informal relationships over the previous focus on hiring expert professionals to run polished segmented programs.

Intergenerational church writers have also pointed to research that suggests that the best way to retain children and young people in the church is to integrate them more from the word go,[3] and to acknowledge the importance of parents and the church's role in supporting them.[4] They have also pointed to the social learning theory of Vygotsky who suggested that people learn best in social settings and alongside people who are ahead of them in developmental terms.[5]

Whether intergenerational church eventually passes as a fad or is taken on by churches as an important foundation for mission and ministry in the twenty-first century, only time will tell. But with all the fresh thinking coming out from intergenerational church writers it is certainly something worth thinking about! ∎

THINK

What examples can you think of that have demonstrated the importance of intergenerational relationships in your community of faith?

What are the major obstacles in your context to intergenerational formation and, what might be done to overcome them?

What might it mean to beleive that old and young are together brothers and sisters in Christ?

READ

Intergenerational Work and Ministry: Report of the Church of Scotland Guild and National Youth Assembly to the General Assembly of the Church of Scotland, 2017.

Philip Mounstephen and Kelly Martin, **Body Beautiful: Recapturing a Vision for All-age Church,** (Cambridge: Grove Booklets, 2004)

Jason Gardner, **Mend the Gap – Can the church the church reconnect the Generations,** (Nottingham: IVP, 2008)

Holly C. Allen and Christine L. Ross, **Intergenerational Christian Formation - Bringing the Whole Church Together in Ministry, Community and Worship,** (Illinois: IVP, 2012)

AOT

In his book, Mend the Gap, Jason Gardner has several useful ideas to try out. One that is particularly helpful is setting up an Intergenerational working group - a body made up of a person from each generation in the church - to discuss options and ideas for bringing the generations together. Why not consider setting up one such group in your church?

RESOURCE

Explore Together from Scripture Union is a helpful resource for running activities and worship services along intergenerational lines www.exploretogether.org

Ed Mackenzie and Gareth Crispin, **Together with God: an introduction to family worship**, (Birmingham: Morse-Brown Publishing, 2016)

Close to Home resources from the Presbyterian Church in Ireland including videos, a booklet and a Dvd, www.presbyterianireland.org/closetohome

3. See: S. K. Galgay, *Solving the retention problem through integration: A communal Vision for Youth Ministry,* Journal of Youth Ministry, 11(1) and M. Nel, *The Inclusive Congregational Approach to Youth Ministry* in Mark H. Senter (ed), Four views of Youth Ministry and the Church (Grand Rapids: Zondervan, 2001), p.1-22

4. See: Chap Clark, & Kara E. Powell, *Sticky Faith - Everyday ideas to build lasting faith in your kids* (Grand Rapids: Zondervan, 2011) and Jason Gardner, *Mend the Gap – Can the Church Reconnect the Generations* (Nottingham: IVP, 2008), p.163-190

5. Holly C. Allen and Christine L. Ross, *Intergenerational Christian Formation - Bringing the Whole Church Together in Ministry, Community and Worship* (Illinois: IVP, 2012), p.98-102

TO INCLUSION AND BEYOND
(ADDITIONAL SUPPORT NEEDS)

Mark Arnold

Additional Needs Ministry Director, Urban Saints

I n Scotland 24.9% of school pupils in 2016 had additional support needs (ASN), of which 60% were boys.[6] The figures are similar in England, where one in five children have a special education need or disability, ranging from dyslexia to a physical impairment.[7] Those with ASN, and their families, can find life isolating and lonely, with children, siblings and parents often feeling excluded from a wide range of social activities[8], including church.

Let's think for a moment about what church is like for a seven-year-old with autism, who finds that loud, crowded rooms full of bright lights and a range of different smells (coffee, perfume etc) overload their senses and cause them to collapse into a meltdown. Or what it is like for an eleven-year-old with dyslexia, who finds that the beautiful photos that are the backdrop to the words on the screen mean that the words swirl before their eyes. Or what it is like for the fifteen-year-old who uses a wheelchair, when the worship leader says "Let's stand to worship!". As everyone is now standing in front of them they can't see the words to the worship song and as they can't stand, does that mean they can't worship? It is easy to see how people with experiences like this may feel that Church is not for them.

Inclusion

Churches are beginning to take note of these issues and, in many cases, are seeking ways to include children and young people with additional support needs. Quiet spaces are being created with resources the seven-year-old can use to access the service, and the family is encouraged to come in once the rest of the congregation has settled down. A screen with plain backgrounds has been set up for the eleven-year-old and others to access. The fifteen-year-old has been given a choice of places to go that all have line of sight to the screen and the words spoken have been changed to include the phrase "if you are able".

> ## " Let's think for a moment what church is like for a 7-year-old with autism...

In beginning this process, many have found that the best first step to enable inclusion to become a reality rather than an aspiration is to appoint someone to *own* inclusion. If nobody owns it, it's nobody's responsibility to ensure that it happens, and it ends up remaining something to do another day. Such an Inclusion Champion doesn't need to have an extensive education, health, or social care background (although this can sometimes help). What they need most is a heart to help and support the children, young people and families with ASN, and a willingness to try to enable the whole congregation to see what happens in church through their eyes.

Inclusion provides the practical changes necessary for someone to be physically present, to have a space at the table, maybe even to have someone to help them; however, if we just leave things there, we are doing little more than childminding... there is so much more that we can do!

Belonging

Belonging is when someone feels that they aren't just there because someone has ticked a few boxes (ramp ✓, toilet ✓, helper ✓), but they are there because they are *wanted*; they feel they can *contribute* something, and that their contribution is *valued*. Belonging happens when a church looks beyond the disability and sees the person, sees the personality, the skills and gifts, rather than the ASN.

Belonging happens when the child or young person, and their family, feel *at home*.

This is a congregational journey to be spearheaded by the leadership but needing everyone to participate:

1. How are those with additional support needs given opportunities to serve?

2. How are the gifts, skills and talents of those with additional support needs recognised?

3. When are the views and opinions of those with disability, or their families, sought?

Belonging is about building a relationship, an affinity, with each person, so that they feel secure and accepted for who they are. When that point is reached, the next stage of the journey, spiritual development, then becomes a natural progression.

Spiritual development

If a child or young person with ASN truly belongs to the church family, then we naturally want the very best for them. We want to help them to take steps of faith, to grow in their understanding of God, and to grow as disciples, just as we would for anyone else. This will probably look different for each individual, but it should be our fundamental aim to grow and develop *everyone's* faith and equip each person to pass it on to others.

Jesus showed us that the person and their salvation are more important than their disability. The paralysed man lowered through the roof by his friends was forgiven for his sins first, and healed of his paralysis second (Luke 5.17-26). In the 'Parable of the Great Banquet', Jesus shows that all are invited to the feast of heaven (Luke 14.15-24). In the 'Great Commission' he shows that we are to take the Good News to everyone, everywhere; there are no exceptions (Mark 16.15-18).

The three steps we've looked at together should be steps we take with *everyone* we reach out to, regardless of their disability/ASN: including children and young people with ASN by making what we do accessible, helping them to feel that they really belong, and are valued for who they are and what they contribute, and taking care to help them to grow and develop spiritually. Will you help take these steps in your church? ■

THINK

Explore in the Bible the times that Jesus connected with people with disabilities; how did he treat them and how did he expect others to treat them? Think about how these encounters can teach us to think differently about disability.

How can you look beyond the disability or ASN to see the person, and how will you help them to belong?

How can you help develop and grow the faith of the children and young people with additional support needs in your church and community, releasing and using their God-given skills, gifts and talents?

READ

theadditionalneedsblogfather.wordpress.com

John Gillibrand, **Disabled Church – Disabled Society**, (London: Jessica Kingsley Publishers, 2010)

Deborah Brownson, **He's Not Naughty! – A Child's Guide to Autism,** (Barrow-In-Furness: Bodhi Book Press, 2014)

Kathleen Muldoon, **Yes I Can! – A Kid's Guide to Dealing with Physical Challenges,** (St. Meinrad, Indiana: One Caring Place, Abbey Press, 2010)

Jesus showed us that the person and their salvation are more important than their disability..

ACT

Speak to those in your congregation or others you know who have ASN. What are their experiences of church?

Consider appointing an Inclusion Champion in your church. If your church is part of the Church of Scotland speak to your Learning Disabilities Contact Person.

Access some further training to help you get started. Urban Saints provide a training evening called 'All Inclusive?' and other training options are also available.

Connect with others who are on the same journey. A vibrant group called the Additional Needs Alliance www.additionalneedsalliance.org.uk includes hundreds of children's/youth workers, parents and representatives of disability organisations, all of whom are passionate about this ministry area. Some may be near you.

RESOURCE

Irene Smale, **Multi-Sensory Ideas for Worship,** (Eastbourne: Kingsway Communications, 2009)

Tara Delaney, **101 Games and Activities for Children with Autism, Asperger's, and Sensory Processing Disorders,** (USA: McGraw-Hill, 2010)

Urban Saints - Additional Needs support **www.urbansaints.org/additionalneeds**

Learning Disabilities: A discussion starter (Church of Scotland) www.churchofscotland.org.uk/learn

Learning Disabilities: Action Pack (Church of Scotland) www.churchofscotland.org.uk/connect/learning_disabilities

6. http://www.gov.scot/Topics/Statistics/Browse/School-Education/TrendSpecialEducation [accessed 24th January 2017]

7. *Reforms for children with SEN and disabilities come into effect* (2014) www.gov.uk/government/news/reforms-for-children-with-sen-and-disabilities-come-into-effect [accessed 17th November 2016]

8. *Mumsnet parents: negative attitudes are holding back our disabled children* (2014) www.scope.org.uk/About-Us/Media/Press-releases/February-2014/Mumsnet-parents-negative-attitudes-are-holding-back [accessed 17th November 2016]

CHILDREN, YOUNG PEOPLE AND BAPTISM

Paul Nimmo

King's Chair of Systematic Theology, University of Aberdeen

A t the end of the Gospel of Matthew, Jesus commands his followers to "Go ... and make disciples of all nations, baptising them in the name of the Father and of the Son and of the Holy Spirit" (Matthew 28.19). Since the earliest days of the Church, and in obedience to that command, the practice of baptism has marked an important point in the Christian journey of faith. Indeed, for many in the Church of Scotland, it will have marked their very first step in the Christian life, for they will have been baptised as infants, for others, it will have involved a conscious decision of faith made at a later point in their lives.

Received in community

Common to the baptism of adults and children is the idea that in undergoing baptism we are received into the community of the church. This is demonstrated not only in terms of the formal words of welcome spoken in the course of the sacrament of baptism, but also in terms of the public act of welcome that takes place through the presence and participation of the congregation. The purpose of our baptism is to offer us reassurance that our sins are forgiven, and to represent our coming to new life in being united with Jesus Christ. The result is that in our baptism we are recognised as being children of God.

Differing views

In the history of the Church, the understanding of baptism has not been without controversy. One of the major debates about baptism has been about the baptism of infants and young children.

On the one hand, New Testament accounts of baptism often indicate explicitly that faith is present before baptism (as in Acts 8.12 and 18.8). This suggests that the baptism of the very young may not be justified, as they cannot be said to have faith in an explicit or conscious way. Moreover, it is often remarked that Scripture gives no explicit command or account to baptise children, with the closest example being ambiguous references to the baptism of households (see Acts 16.15 and 1 Corinthians 1.16). And it is sometimes feared that the practice of baptising infants and young children may devalue the grace of God and obscure the link between baptism and discipleship.

On the other hand, the covenant between God and God's people seems always to include children and young people (see Genesis 17.7 and Acts 2.39). Jesus, indeed, offers a particular welcome to children, saying 'Whoever welcomes one such child in my name welcomes me' (Matthew 18.5). Baptism is a sign of God's covenant with us, giving us a new marker of belonging to God in place of the Old Testament practice of circumcision (see Colossians 2.11–12). In this way, the baptism of infants and young children is a wonderful sign of the way in which the grace of God always comes to meet us before we move to recognise it, and it is nowhere forbidden in Scripture.

The sacrement of baptism also offers children and young people a particular occasion on which to conside their own Christian journey.

The Church of Scotland continues to affirm and support the practice of infant baptism. However, recent conversations in the Church have led to the provision of liturgical materials for those who prefer to have infants blessed or dedicated in the Church instead of being baptised, leaving open the possibility for those infants to request baptism for themselves in later years.

The whole family of God

In all events, the sacrament of baptism is an occasion of Christian witness. In the case of infants and young children, the parent(s) or guardian(s) are called upon to acknowledge their own Christian faith, and to promise to raise the children in the life and worship of the church. Young people and adults who are being baptised are required to profess their Christian faith, and to promise to serve God and continue in the community of the church. The congregation also has a crucial role to play: they are asked to say together the words of the Apostles' Creed, and to commit to living in a Christian way and to sharing the knowledge and love of Jesus Christ with others.

In this way, baptism is about far more than one person. It is an event that involves the whole family of God in a service of celebration – rejoicing in the new person being welcomed formally into the church and rejoicing in the great blessings of God of which the sacrament of baptism is a sign. The promises being taken by those closest to the font – the parent(s) or guardian(s) of the infant or the adults being themselves baptised – are in no sense more important than those being taken by those in the pews: in baptism, the whole community is drawn together in a renewal of faith, purpose and direction in their Christian discipleship.

The sacrament of baptism also offers children and young people a particular occasion on which to consider their own Christian journey. They can be encouraged in light of the service they have seen to reflect on their own journey in the church: about when it started, about who was involved, and about what they have experienced and learned later on the way. And they can also be encouraged to think about the event of baptism itself: about what the water of baptism symbolises, about what the promises of baptism mean, and about what becoming and being a Christian means. Finally, they can be encouraged to think through why we speak of baptism as a 'celebration'. ■

THINK

Why might it be important for Christians to be baptised?

Why might it be controversial for infants to be baptised?

How can children and young people be made to feel part of a baptismal service?

Consider how your congregation can be encouraged and empowered to carry out the promises they make during baptismal services.

READ

The sections on baptism in the Scots Confession (Articles XXI–XXIII) or in the Westminster Confession (Chapters XXVII–XXVIII) give a helpful outline of the understanding of baptism that has been normative in the history of the Church of Scotland.

ACT

Next time there is a baptism celebrated in the congregation, why not think through with children and young people the different parts of the sacrament – the movement involved, the words spoken, the promises made – in order to consider what each part might mean or signify, and how it might relate to everyone present in the congregation?

RESOURCE

Craig Cameron, **The Baptism Cube,** (Church House Publishing, 2006)

Diana Murrie, **My Baptism Book: a child's guide to baptism,** (Church House Publishing, 2012)

Richard Burge, Penny Fuller and Mary Hawes, **My Baptism Journey: Activity Book,** (Barnabas for Children, 2014)

Richard Burge, Penny Fuller and Mary Hawes, **Getting Ready for Baptism Course Book,** (Barnabas for Children, 2014)

CHILDREN, YOUNG PEOPLE AND COMMUNION

Gayle Taylor

Associate Minister (Children and Youth) of Colinton Parish Church

Communion in the Church of Scotland

When I prepared to officiate at my first communion after ordination, I remember my session clerk presenting me with a diagram of how communion was served in that church. It was like a military operation – common cup, individual cups, alcoholic, non-alcoholic and two teams of six, three teams of two and so on! "Is this really what Jesus intended? I asked. Of course, logistically if 200 people need to be served you can see how it gets this way but could we have communion in smaller groups? Could we provide a choice and resources to help put people at ease?

My own understanding of communion rooted in my theological training and Church of Scotland experience is shaped around three core beliefs about God. **Eternal** – God is beyond time and so the connection we have spiritually at the table of our Lord is not just with those there in the present but with those gone before us and those yet to come (the communion of saints). **Embodied** – Although a sacrament is a mystery with a meaning beyond words, the body of Christ is present through the bread and in the gathered congregation sanctified by God. **Exclusive** – it is not ours, it is not about what we do but what God does - God's grace, Christ's table. So the invitation is inclusive, the gifts of God are offered to all for us to graciously receive.

The sacraments involve the whole family of God

In the Church of Scotland we have two sacraments and children are certainly included in baptism! In fact, as we talk about infant baptism, perhaps we could also think of infant communion, moving beyond the idea that people need to be taught and tested before they are admitted to the table. Maybe, the parents, the family of the church, the village that it takes to raise a child, could do what they do at baptisms and model the essence of the sacrament beyond a cerebral understanding. Sacraments are sensual; Jesus chose very ordinary elements of water, wine and bread as symbols because they are so accessible to us every day. However, they become special as we set them apart for a spiritual and holy use - a mystery we connect with at communion due to the way we prepare and approach the table.

When I was about seven years old, I remember my Gran teaching me how to set the table for a big family meal. There was quite a lot to it in those days! The fork on the left, the knife on the right, a soup spoon on the side of the knife and a desert spoon along the top of the table mat/place setting. There were also side plates and butter knives and glasses, oh, and at Christmas, there was a cracker to pull with your neighbour! My point is, I remember: I know how to set the table because as a child my Gran took time to show me and to tell me why we needed all the things and then, I saw them all in action later on - the learning and the doing connected.

Being at the table wasn't always easy because it was a tight squeeze and actually it looked neater and prettier when no one was sitting at it! Oh, and for a time, there was a children's table! with smaller, age appropriate things on it, where

the cousins enjoyed a bit of mischief but where the older cousins began to feel it was not fair looking up at the big table, with the wine on it, which they were not ready for just yet.

My Gran taught me how to set the table and while we were doing it, I learnt that there was a place for me. This made the eating and sharing a feast for the senses - taste and sight, touch and smell and sound round that table. We had all we needed and were immersed in family. That to me is sacramental - a sacred moment beyond words, using the senses evoking deeper understanding and involving the whole family.

Beginning the journey of including children and young people in communion

Think of the children and young people in your life and what you would like to share with them. If they were hungry and wanted to sit with you and spend time with you creating a way of being and a sense of belonging, what would you say? What is your agenda? How do the rules we have built up get in the way of the nurture and nourishment we can offer to children and young people as they grow in faith?

A family meal is often idealised in the planning and messy in reality. Provision and practicalities are of course necessary factors in our preparation but often we have developed practices out of the cultural norms of the time or out of our own preferences around what we can tolerate. In our church café recently when I asked for some toys to be put out for some small children who were visiting, a church elder said to me "In my day, children were seen and not heard". My response, kindly, was "well, this is a different day".

You may have a separate children's table/activity. This may suit you but on the other hand your church may be mourning the fact that it has no children on a Sunday. You may have become so used to how you do communion that no one has asked for a long, long time about why you do it that way. Children are very good at asking questions and bringing children into something is a gift to our perspective, causing us to deconstruct our own practice so we can explain the meaning to them. I believe this is rooted in Jesus' ministry: Jesus told the disciples not to exclude the children from a time of blessing but placed children in the middle of things and said "Whoever does not receive the kingdom like a little child will never enter it" (Luke 18.15).

So let's allow, as Jesus suggests, children to help us understand! And then, there's something about being the Gran – the adult who can take time, preparing thoughtfully and lovingly (as you would for any family gathering) and in that, explaining that the food in itself is not why we're there. The important thing is that we gather. We come together, we receive each other, just as we receive the body and blood of Christ. I've always explained communion as 'the union of the community' for this reason. ■

> " **In my day, children were seen and not heard. My response, kindly, was "well, this is a different day"**

THINK

What practicalities and practices do you have for communion in your church and how does this connect to the purpose of the sacrament?

Why and when did children and young people become integrated into the sacrament in your church? If they aren't, was this a conscious decision?

What kind of difference would it make if you were to think about what we could learn and notice by having children and young people in our midst at communion?

READ

The Participation of Baptised Children in the Sacrament of the Lord's Supper, Section 3.11 of the Report of the Board of Education to the General Assembly of the Church of Scotland, 1991

Joyce A. Mercer, **Welcoming Children: a practical theology of childhood,** (Missouri: Chalice Press, 2005)

Steve Pearce and Diana Murrie, **Children and Holy Communion,** (Church House Publishing, 1997)

ACT

Just as you seek to make the church more welcoming in general, what kinds of things would make it easier for young families to share in communion? Perhaps a high chair so little ones can join in and eat a snack while everyone else gets something? What about laminated picture or symbols on a sheet that show what to do at communion for children and also others who don't read or who have other additional support needs. Could you do a survey?

RESOURCE

Margaret Withers, **Welcome to the Lord's table,** (Barnabas for Children, 2013)

Kathleen Crawford, **My Communion Book: a child's guide to holy communion,** (Church House Publishing, 2010)

Nick Harding, **Ready to Share One Bread: preparing children for holy communion,** (SPCK, 2015)

My Story

Darren Phillip

Youth and Children's Development Worker, Livingston United Parish Church

When I joined the team at Livingston United Parish Church, the preacher at my Service of Introduction joked, "If you want to upset the congregation, move the furniture... or change the way Communion is served." It was with more than a little trepidation, then, that we decided to do both.

The congregation had embarked on an intentionally intergenerational way of being, with a new style of worship where all ages could fully participate together. Teams from a cross-section of the congregation began to meet to prepare and lead worship that included a balance of words, symbols, movement, participative action, contemplation and music, each designed so that the youngest and the oldest alike could take part. This half-hour service quickly became one of my most fulfilling experiences of church: watching a six-year-old boy help an elderly lady mould her prayer in clay, hearing the usually shy middle-aged man quietly sharing his story of faith with a teenager, seeing the youngest (six months) and the oldest (ninety-eight years) come forward for baptism.

Soon, though, the time came to consider how this intergenerational community should celebrate the Sacrament of Holy Communion. This led me to think about my own earliest memories of Communion, and I realised that I didn't really have any. In my childhood experience of church, the Lord's Supper was strictly off-limits. All I knew was that if we turned up and there was a white cloth on the table, all of the children would be going out to the hall for some colouring-in. As I was reaching the end of primary school, we were taken onto the church balcony to watch the celebration of Communion taking place, but it was made very clear that we were not welcome to participate. Many of us struggled, even then, to understand this – if we were part of the family of the church, why were we not allowed to sit at the family meal?

With an intergenerational commitment, things would have to be different in Livingston. We took inspiration from the Jewish celebration of Passover where the story is told through the youngest asking questions and the oldest answering them. We moved most of the furniture out of the way, sat on cushions on the floor and shared the story of the Lord's Supper by asking and answering questions together, with adults and children learning from one another.

Welcoming children to share in this feast has been a huge blessing. On one occasion, a three-year-old girl was serving the wine and as she handed each glass to its recipient, she pulled her skirt over her head, danced in a twirl and shouted, 'Hooray!' One pre-school boy likes to shout out as he finishes the bread, 'God is good!' To such as these belongs the kingdom of heaven...

Many older members of the congregation have spoken of how their experience and understanding of the Sacrament has been changed by the presence, questioning, sharing, joy and challenge that children have brought to the table. It is proving to be a formative experience for children too, with some of the children involved in worship planning asking to celebrate it more often. The mystery, symbolism and communal act of sharing that is involved in breaking bread and drinking wine together draw all ages closer to God, and the family of God is made more complete by all God's children meeting round the table. ∎

My Story

André du Plessis

Volunteer at St Columba's Parish Church, Aberdeen

I am a volunteer at church and church-run events for children and young people. My volunteering mostly involves lending a hand wherever I can to the leaders, so I am less involved in the "upfront" activities and more involved on a one-to-one basis, building relationships with individuals and small groups.

My reason for getting involved with children and young people's ministry is fairly simple – I wanted to tell them about Jesus. I'm blessed to have been brought up in a Christian family and have therefore been learning from the Bible about God and Jesus from a young age. I wanted to share this privilege with other children and young people. Jesus' love for children is clear in the Bible; they are so precious to him (as we all are!) and although these children and young people don't get to sit with Jesus as some of the children mentioned in the Bible did, they can get to know him personally and for me anything that encourages this has to be a good thing.

It would be dishonest of me to claim that I made the step into volunteering for children's ministry myself. It was mostly through being asked by others that I became involved. However, I am grateful for that and it is something that I find joyful, encouraging and challenging. Children and young people ask the most wonderful, challenging questions and I find that this challenges me when I look at some of the stories in the Bible. When I have had the opportunity to prepare a story, really considering what it is about and what it teaches, it has often led me to having a much greater understanding and appreciation of the story than I previously thought I did.

The church is everybody, no matter what age, and it is wonderful when you see children and young people being included and getting involved in church. I believe one great way of including children and young people and 'Being Church Together' is allowing them to get involved in some of the everyday activities of church such as playing in the worship band, helping to present the song lyrics on the screens, and even putting away the chairs after the service where I worship we have a four-year-old who is always very keen to help put them away! Although this is not a 'teaching and learning together' event as such, it helps to make them feel included and involved, and to realise that, rather than just being led by adults, they are contributing themselves. It helps them to know they are part of the church family and that they make a difference, rather than being a separate entity that just tags on to the 'adult church'. It helps them to build relationships with adult Christians, beneficial to both parties in growing in faith. It is crucial that children and young people know they are an essential part of church and it is everyone's responsibility to ensure that they are encouraged to feel this way. ■

WORKING TOGETHER

CHURCH LEADERSHIP

Tony Stephen

Minister of Banchory Ternan West Parish Church

My name is Tony Stephen and I am the minister for the West Church in Banchory, Aberdeenshire. When I describe my job, I first point people back to the roots of the word minister - one who serves. The kind of leadership I feel called to is a servant leadership. One of the first things that our Kirk Session did, following my arrival, was to sit down and ask some basic questions about our role as elders in our local church. As we studied together we saw that the model of servant leaders - elders, overseers or shepherds, those given responsibility of oversight over groups of believers - is rooted in Scripture.

Leadership in the Bible

Moses was urged to select capable people from among all the people who feared God, trustworthy people who hated dishonest gain, and he appointed them as officials over thousands, hundreds, fifties and tens (Exodus 18.21). In the early Church these office bearers were known as elders, deacons, shepherds, bishops or overseers; and the qualities expected of elders included being full of the Spirit, and wisdom. The aim, and perhaps a measure of the effectiveness of such a body of elders, seemed to be that local communities of Jesus' followers would be strengthened in faith, and growing in numbers (Acts 16.4-5). So, local groups of elders, or overseers, were responsible for the care and spiritual health of local congregations, for establishing new congregations, for spreading the gospel, for good planning, and for exercising a variety of gifts to build up the body of believers for works of service. The local church community did not exist for its own benefit, of course. God had not created his people to form a cosy club of the saved, but for works of service, to join in with the work that God had made them for, to join in with God's action in the world, to be part of a blessing machine, a blessing movement, a blessing community.

In the New Testament, this leadership responsibility was not individualised in a charismatic hero figure, but rather the group took a collective responsibility to serve the community's basic needs. This servant leadership could only be provided by a plurality of people, a team, a body, with a variety of gifts. There are no Biblical models of the omni-competent leader.

A community of faith

The local church is a community of faith; a community that passes on the faith to the next generation. A local church that does not engage meaningfully with younger generations is a local church that has no future. The Church of Scotland structures have traditionally charged the minister and Kirk Session with responsibility for discipleship within the congregation, including children and young people, and for appointing volunteers, providing access to training, and implementing the church's policy on safeguarding. The congregation takes vows at baptism to attend to the Christian upbringing of children. This implies to us that as the whole people of God we all share these responsibilities. We are all engaged with children and young people to some extent. The question is not whether we engage with children and young people, but instead what sort of quality of engagement we are having.

In my experience, healthy church communities put a priority on engaging with children and young people, often investing time and salaries in those who will have specific ministries to children and young people; an investment that provides lasting fruit. I believe those doing specific ministry with children and young people need to be central to our leadership structures, to be included in discerning how best to join in with what God is doing in our local community, and to be supported and encouraged by our leadership structures. If we are a community of faith that passes on the faith, then those more specifically involved in supporting and coordinating children and youth ministry are a crucial part of our church leadership.

Sharing in servant leadership

I believe that if we are to be a community of faith that passes on the faith, we have to be able to share our servant leadership. If we are to follow the example of Paul in the New Testament, then our ministers and elders need to be able to take risks and give responsibility to each generation, to allow people to find their gifts, to remember that we were young and inexperienced leaders once, and that it was and is OK to make mistakes, and even to fail at times.   Each generation should be given trust and responsibility from the start, to be able to expand their areas of gifting. And for that current leaders may need to make room, stand aside, or step back at times, and to hand over the keys.

In my own context, our Kirk Session and our shared Youth Project encourage young leaders in a variety of ways - our internships are a great example. Our current salaried youth workers were members of the youth group, then later returned as interns, and are now ministering with us full-time and passing on their servant leadership to others. Many of the young people and interns who have been part of this project are now serving in various types of leadership across the world.

In all of this, relationships are crucial. The Biblical model is sharing life, telling stories, sharing the difficult as well as the easy things.   And we would be foolish to underestimate prayer, and the need to pray for new and young leaders, for each generation.   We have gradually realised that we should fan into flame their gifts rather than hogging the limelight ourselves. It is a long and often messy process. We have certainly made plenty of mistakes but our church is all the better for it. ■

THINK

Have there been any people in your life who have exhibited servant leadership? How can you encourage servant leadership in your church context? Do any of your structures need to change?

How are those involved in leadership with children and young people also involved in wider church decisions?

Consider how you are investing in children and youth leaders (resources, training, enabling, celebrating, including etc).

READ

Developing the Eldership, Appendix III of the Report of the Mission and Discipleship Council to the General Assembly of the Church of Scotland, 2017

Kara Powell, Jake Mulder and Brad Griffin, **Growing Young: 6 essential strategies to help young people discover and love your church,** (Grand Rapids: Baker Books, 2016), Particularly chapter 2

Chap Clark et al, **Adoptive Youth Ministry: integrating emerging generations into the family of faith,** (Grand Rapids: Baker Academic, 2016), Particularly chapters 19 and 22

Andrew Root, **Bonhoeffer as Youth Worker: a theological vision for discipleship and life together,** (Grand Rapids: Baker Academic, 2014)

ACT

Invite those involved in leadership with children and young people to a Kirk Session meeting to share vision.

Consider how you can make engaging with children and young people a priority for your church leadership.

RESOURCE

David Plews (ed.), **Learn: Eldership,** (Edinburgh: Saint Andrew Press, 2015)

www.churchofscotland.org.uk/resources/ office_bearers

REACHING AND KEEPING VOLUNTEERS

Sue Thomson
Schools Worker, Ten Must Know Bible Stories Project

*V*olunteers are vital to our churches! Not to fill the slots on our rotas but because they bring an energy, an enthusiasm and fresh ideas to our ministries. They bring unique individual gifts that strengthen and widen our ministries. Volunteers create teams, teams create sustainability and teams are fun!

It is crucial to our churches that we give people the chance to volunteer and serve. As people serve, their faith matures. They are learning to work alongside others, to relate to people as Jesus would; they are seeing others' faith in action; they will witness answers to prayers; they're getting opportunities to share their faith and they're learning alongside the children and young people. As we work in teams in our churches, friendships are developed and unity is strengthened. Volunteers are vital!

So how do we encourage people to volunteer?
The key thing is to ask them! People don't know about all the opportunities available if you don't tell them about them. But don't just ask them. Tell them stories about the ministry, share your hopes for the future, share how God has led you to this point. *Help them grasp the vision you have.* Then invite them to be part of it.

This can be shared 'upfront' in services so everyone hears about the opportunities - this gives people you would never have thought to ask the chance to volunteer. But also make personal requests. These are a real encouragement to the people you ask as they realise you think they'd be good at this role and you're placing value on them and their skills.

Ask God to show you who to ask. You may be surprised who he chooses. You're not looking for experts - you're looking for people whose love for Jesus gives them a humble attitude, a willingness to serve and a faithfulness in prayer. A love for working with children and young people is helpful but many of our volunteers wouldn't initially pick that area as a favourite thing to do. Instead, recognising the importance of ministering

It is crucial to our churches that we give people the chance to volunteer and serve

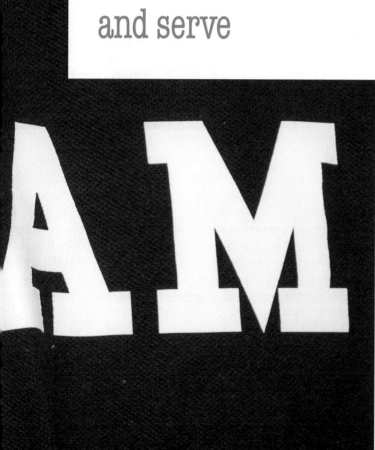

with children and young people may mean they choose to work outside their comfort zone. These people may start by filling vital roles "behind the scenes", e.g. helping with refreshments, but gradually find themselves engaging with the children and young people and loving it!

Consider all ages for your volunteers. Older generations bring experience and wisdom while younger adults are often more prepared to take risks. Young people themselves have many skills that can enhance our ministries and serving and being given responsibility is crucial to their faith development.

Be clear about what you're asking people to volunteer for. What will the role be? Are you asking them to just come along to help or to fulfil a certain role? How much time will they need to commit to each month and for how long? Don't forget to include preparation time and meeting time. Ensure they know that they'll need to go through your Safeguarding procedures.

I have my volunteers, what's next?

Value them and encourage them. Give thanks for them. Ensure they are introduced to the team and children or young people. Keep sharing the vision. Remind them why they're serving and who they're serving. Be the one who serves them. Offer them a week off when you know they're struggling with something. Take them round a bunch of flowers. Say thank you. Write them cards at Christmas with personal messages showing you've noticed their hard work and pointing out where you have

seen God working in and through them. Arrange social occasions for the team. Thank them in public. Make sure their volunteering is recognised within the wider church community. Why not commission the team during a service, encouraging them to share with the congregation what God is doing and then pray for them.

Listen to them. Ask them where they are seeing God at work. Ask them what has been challenging. Have team meetings where you pray and dream together. Let them know their thoughts on the ministry are valued. Use all the things you hear from your volunteers to plan the future direction of the ministry. Better still, plan it together. Why not invite them to a Kirk Session meeting?

Let them try. Ensure your ministry is a safe place for your volunteers to try out gifts and skills. Our gifts grow with practise. Let your volunteers practice. Remember everything doesn't need to be perfect for God to be at work.

Have clear expectations. When should they arrive? What do they need to have prepared? What should they be doing during the ministry?

Remember they are volunteers. They have other commitments. Give them as much preparation time as possible and avoid last minute changes.

Train them. By committing to ensure volunteers are properly trained you are showing that you value them. Be on the lookout for conferences and training courses they can attend. Ensure the church pays for the cost of these. You could send them articles, recommend books or subscribe to the Youth and Children's Work magazine for them.

What if it's not working?

Don't gossip or complain about your volunteers. Praise God for them even when you're frustrated. If you're really struggling with a volunteer find one wise person to talk to and pray with. Meet with the volunteer and reinforce expectations. Ask them if they're enjoying the role. Ask them whether there is something else going on in their lives that is affecting their role in your team. Identify where they are succeeding and provide opportunities for them to do more of that. Pray for them. ■

THINK

How can you prioritise your own relationship with God?

What support is available for volunteers in your congregation?

How easy would it be for someone in your congregation to stop volunteering without feeling like they were letting people down?

READ

Martin Saunders, **Youth Work from Scratch: how to launch or revitalize a church youth project,** (Oxford: Monarch Books, 2013)

Karla Yaconelli, **Getting Fired for the Glory of God: collected words of Mike Yaconelli for youth workers,** (Grand Rapids: Youth Specialties, 2008)

ACT

Organise a meal out for your team of volunteers.

Invite the team to share photos and stories of their ministry in a service. Then invite the elders (and/or the children and young people!) to pray for them.

Invite a team of volunteers to a Kirk Session meeting, giving them space to share the highlights and difficulties of their ministry and any ideas they have for the wider church and then pray together.

RESOURCE

Doug Fields, **Youth Leader Training on the Go**, (Colorado: Group Publishing, 2006)

www.weloveouryouthworker.org.uk

Volunteer Scotland www.volunteerscotland.net

BEING AN EFFECTIVE VOLUNTEER

Vicky Stigant
Youth Work Facilitator for Gordon Presbytery

As someone who works with children and young people in the Church at a presbytery level, I rely on a great many volunteers who give freely of their time, talents and resources to see children and young people grow in their faith. Very little of the great work that is done in churches could happen without volunteers and I am constantly humbled by people who turn up after a hard day at work, excited about welcoming a group of young people for the evening. The kingdom of God is made known in many ways and one of them is the faithful ministry of the people of God to God's children.

The reasons why we volunteer vary, are often complex, and change over time. We may want to give something back to a community that has helped us learn new skills and improve our CV, or we may feel that we have a duty to volunteer.[9] Within the church, many volunteers are motivated by their own faith and see what they are doing to help children and young people grow in their own faith as a calling. In an ideal world, what motivates us to volunteer and what we are doing in volunteering, match up well and we find the work fun, engaging and rewarding.

Volunteers bring many different qualities to a ministry with children and young people. By definition, volunteers are not there because they are paid to be, but because they want to be. They bring gifts, skills and a wide range of experience which opens up new possibilities for the children they work with.[10]

However, sometimes work with children and young people can be tough and we don't always feel that we are being effective in what we are doing. There can be many reasons for this. Groups change over time and what was once so full of life may now be struggling, or doesn't give us the opportunity to use our God-given gifts. Sometimes, we find ourselves working with children whose needs we can't meet. Sometimes, we are just tired and don't feel like we are able to commit as much time and energy as a group needs.

It can be really helpful to make sure there are practices built in to your volunteering, both as an individual and team, that help you to sustain it in long term.

Be a disciple first

Make sure that you prioritise your own relationship with God. It is God who called you into this ministry and God who sustains you. It is all too easy to find ourselves only picking up the Bible to prepare for Sunday school, but our ministry begins with our own relationship with God.[11] That could mean setting aside time to pray, meeting up with others for a Bible study, or just arranging the rota so that sometimes you go to church just to worship and not to run anything. It will look different for each of us because we all connect with God in different ways.

Connect

Wherever possible, try to create teams of people to work together. This might mean just the two or three of you that run a particular group, or you may be able to build a bigger team, including people that run other groups within your congregation or within other churches. This will help you to find support and encouragement and benefit from the gifts of many different people when it comes to planning and running work.

Be deliberate about building bridges between work with children and young people and the wider congregation. Encourage your congregation

to pray for the children and young people (and the children and young people to pray for the adults). Be on the lookout for who else God might be calling to come and volunteer.

Find opportunities for training and development

Just as we are helping our children and young people to learn more about God, we too can learn new things. It is good to find opportunities to learn and grow, both in our own faith and also in the skills we bring to our volunteering. New ideas and approaches can keep what we are doing fresh and help us feel equipped to respond to the needs of those you serve.

Evaluate

It is helpful to take time to evaluate what we are doing, both individually and as a team. Asking critical questions about the groups and projects we have invested in can be tough, but it enables us to question whether what we are doing is effective and to identify areas that need work or change. It also gives us an opportunity to identify and celebrate what God is doing.

Look after yourself

Sometimes, volunteering can begin to feel like a burden. Perhaps your circumstances have changed, leaving you with less time to commit, or you have been doing something for a long time and it is time to take a break. God tells us to take time to rest. Hopefully, other people in your team can step in to share the burden, or because of your links to the wider congregation, new people are feeling called to the work. Sometimes, after a break, you will want to return; at other times you'll find that God is calling you into a new ministry. ∎

THINK

How can you prioritise your own relationship with God?

What support is available for volunteers in your congregation?

How easy would it be for someone in your congregation to stop volunteering without feeling they were letting people down?

READ

Danny Brierly, **What Every Volunteer Youth Worker Should Know,** (Authentic: Carlisle, 2002)

Emlyn Williams, **Reaching and Keeping Volunteers**, (Grove Books Ltd, Cambridge, 2006)

ACT

Why not arrange a time when all the volunteers involved in children's and youth work can come together to share ideas, plan and pray together.

Identify areas where volunteers would benefit from training or support and research ways in which that can be accessed or offered.

Consider attending the next Community of Faith Conference run by the Church of Scotland.

RESOURCE

There are many different organisations in Scotland that offer support and training to volunteers. Nationally, these include Urban Saints, Youth for Christ, Scripture Union Scotland, and, indeed the Church of Scotland.

www.churchofscotland.org.uk/childrenandyouth

9. Joe Saxton, Tim Harrison and Mhairi Guild, *The New Alchemy*, (NFPSynergy, 2015), pp. 35-36

10. Emlyn Williams, *Reaching and Keeping Volunteers*, (Cambridge:Grove Books Ltd, 2006), pp. 8-9

11. Karla Yaconelli (Ed), *Getting Fired For the Glory of God*, (El Cajon: Youth Specialities, 2008), p.126

CHILDREN AND YOUNG PEOPLE AS LEADERS

Jen Robertson
Church/School Youth Development Worker for Hamilton Presbytery

As Presbyterians, we have always welcomed our youngest children into our community of faith through baptism, reminding us that children and young people from birth are included and fully valued in our congregations. Our wider society, led by cognitive development theorists, has over recent years rethought the child's place in political and public life; children are no longer seen as incompetent and incapable of taking part in decisions that affect their lives, but are able to participate fully in them.[12] With this theological commitment to the inclusion of young people, and the cultural context that we now live in, we should be at the forefront of enabling and liberating children and young people to be fully involved in leadership within the church.

In practice, however, this is often not the case, so we need to consider what kind of congregations we need to be for children and young people to have their leadership gifts nurtured and utilised. How can we be places where they are able to lead in a meaningful rather than tokenistic or patronising way?

What makes a leader?

We may have preconceived ideas of leadership that need to be challenged, for if we don't these ideas may prevent young people from developing real skills and having experience of responsibility. What do we consider makes a good leader? Is it someone who commands authority, has confidence, has a vast range of developed skills, qualifications and experiences, is a particular gender and has reached a certain age?

The people Jesus gathered around him to lead the Church after he had ascended to heaven did not meet the standard that ociety had set for leaders. The disciples were undoubtedly young from our twenty-first[st] century perspective, probably around fifteen or sixteen years old and they were not the 'elite' of society.[13] They hadn't made the grade educationally and were not trainee rabbi material, but when Jesus arrived and asked them to follow him that was the life he was calling them to. If Jesus got alongside the young and the 'unexpected' leaders then perhaps we should do the same! These young leaders experienced life with Jesus – conversed with him, ate with him, travelled with him, watched him, laughed and cried with him. They were given work to do, sometimes unsupervised, as Jesus sent them out to proclaim his kingdom (Matthew 10).

Nurturing communities

As we contemplate how our congregations can be places where children and young people can lead, we need to create a similar community to that which Jesus had with his disciples a nurturing community that is of huge significance in young people's lives. Meaningful leadership opportunities will grow and be nurtured only in the right conditions.[14] These conditions are beautifully described by Nick Shepherd in his book Faith Generation, in which he examines case studies of churches that had this depth of community, places where young people's faith was made plausible and they were helped in forming their Christian identity.[15]

Within this type of community children and young people can know and be known and leadership skills discovered and used. In this nurturing context risks can be taken and mistakes made alongside fellow older leaders who will support younger

leaders who are in difficulty and share the pain of error. Rather than seeing themselves as experts, adults need to see themselves as fellow pilgrims who, while having a bit more knowledge and experience, have just as much to learn from the leadership of the younger generations.[16]

Developing gifts and calling

This vision of a rich nurturing community is perhaps in sharp contrast to some of our own experiences of congregations where young people may be left to only lead other younger people, often because there are very few teenagers in the congregation and the 'easy' option is to put them with the younger children as 'leaders'.

If we want to be congregations who have children and young people as leaders then our first job is to work hard to include them and make them an integral part of our congregations. This kind of community means that it will not only be within youth and children's ministry that leadership can develop. Being young does not mean that your gifting or calling will necessarily be in leading children. Young people's leadership can be seen across the wide variety of ministry within our congregations.

For example, in the...

- Finance team - prayerfully directing the stewardship of the congregations giving.

- Pastoral care team - planning and exploring how best to care for all members of the church.

- Worship team - in planning services, preaching, leading prayers and worship.

- Outreach team - creating and implementing plans to connect with the local community.

Growing young

If our congregations truly are places where children and young people belong, places where they can explore their faith and their own calling from God then very naturally the leaders among our young people will emerge and will become included in our leadership structures. Undertaking this journey may mean that our structures need to change and develop, but we surely do not want young people to become as dull as we sometimes are!

The church needs young people to move it on, and to bring life and radicalism, alongside older people with their experiences and insights. Our congregations can seem to be inexorably growing old but we can intentionally grow young! A core way to do this is for adults not to rigidly hold onto the 'keys' of leadership but to willingly release them to the next generation within the kind of community that has been described.[17] ■

12. Ruth Sinclair, *Participation in practice: making it meaningful, effective, and sustainable,* (Children and Society, 2004), p.18

13. Rob Bell, *Nooma: Dust 008,* (Zondervan, 2005)

14. Mark Yacconelli, *Contemplative Youth Ministry,* (Zondervan, 2006), p.141

15. Nick Shepherd, *Faith Generation,* (SPCK: London, 2016), p.144

16. Paul Fenton, *Someone to lean on,* (Scripture Union, 1988)

17. Kara Powell, Jake Mulder and Brad Griffin, *Growing Young,* (Grand Rapids: Baker Books, 2016)

THINK

How significant is your faith community for the young people in your congregation? What could you do to make it more significant, creative, meaningful?

What opportunities for leadership are there for young people in your congregation? Using the list that was started above try and think of four more.

What changes might you need to make to your leadership structures to include young leaders?

READ

Mark Yacconelli, **Contemplative Youth Ministry,** (London: SPCK, 2006)

Nick Shepherd, **Faith Generation,** (London: SPCK, 2016)

Kara Powell Jake Mulder and Brad Griffin, **Growing Young,** (Grand Rapids: Baker Books, 2016)

ACT

Organise a lunch for the Kirk Session and children/young people. Give everyone a place to sit so there is a mix of old and young. Eat and play games together, and think of creative ideas to get everybody of all ages chatting about leadership in your congregation.

Explore different parts of the Bible with children/young people, discussing together what makes a good leader. Consider ways that you are all leaders and ways you can develop leadership opportunities.

Follow this up with an all age 'training' event for those who believe they are called to leadership.

RESOURCE

Growing leaders – youth edition (CPAS)
www.cpas.org.uk/church-resources/growing-leaders-suite/growing-leaders-youth-edition

SU Lead Up camps

Urban Saints Leadership programmes

DEALING WITH FAMILY ISSUES

Kerry Reilly
Chief Executive, YMCA Scotland

The children and young people in our congregations and communities don't exist on their own in a vacuum - they all belong to families. That means that as churches we need to be mindful of the fact that we are dealing with children and young people who may be exposed to a range of family issues – new siblings, divorce, blended families, illness, bereavement, distance, addiction, unemployment etc. Such family issues can be complicated and messy and wonderful and challenging all at the same time. Often as adults, we can find it difficult to discuss deeply personal issues such as grief, relationships and personal trauma with other adults. How then do we begin to approach these issues with children and young people?

Unconditional love

When speaking to people about the YMCA I am often asked, "How do you share the Christian ethos of the YMCA with young people?" My response is always, "through unconditional love". We work with some very challenging and vulnerable young people who have often been deeply affected by their family circumstances and situations that are outwith their control or choice. In order to work with those young people, we need to start by building a relationship with them, based on trust and mutual respect.

In reflecting on the place of hospitality within the church, Diana Butler Bass argues that while many experience congregations in America to be places of strict rules and judgement, God's hospitality makes it clear that we should be different, that we should welcome all.[18] Working with children, young people and their families, within a church setting in the UK, demands nothing less.

Mentoring

As a Christian youth worker, I have witnessed how young people respond to adults when they have the opportunity to build trusting and respectful relationships where they are valued for who they are as individuals. Some of the best support programmes offered to young people dealing with family issues are based around a mentoring model.

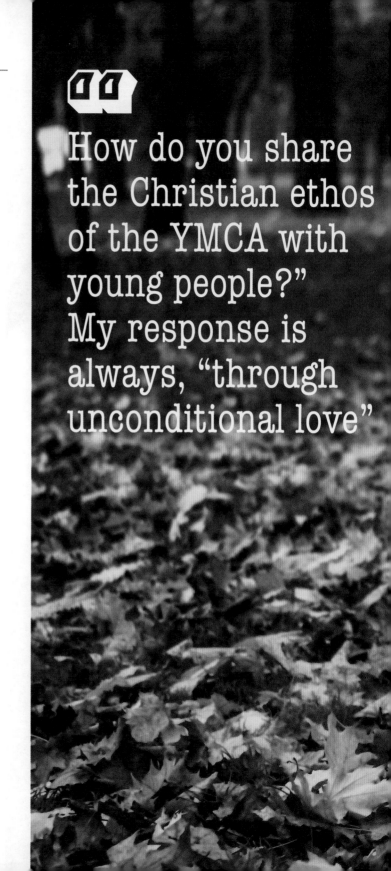

How do you share the Christian ethos of the YMCA with young people?" My response is always, "through unconditional love"

Mentoring provides space where young people have the opportunity to build a trusting relationship with an adult and where they can share and discuss, be listened to and explore solutions to their issues.

In church based work with children and young people, it is sometimes difficult to know how to respond to personal or family issues that a child or young person is facing. In our struggle to know what approach to take it is easy to confuse organizing people with discipling people and thereby substituting informing people for investing in people.[19] There is often a desire to look for the latest programme or initiative that can provide professional support or diversionary activities for young people a tendency to take a Martha rather than a Mary approach and 'do something', even if that 'something' isn't actually what the young person wants or needs.

At times of personal or family challenge, children and young people don't always need activities or programmes. Sometimes, like with a person acting as a mentor, they need supportive relationships with adults, where they are given time to be understood, to be listened to and to be valued, where both the adult and the young person can grow and learn together. Supporting young people is not a one-way process, it is not about teaching or imparting knowledge from one to another; it is about sharing and learning and growing together, deconstructing problems or issues, and building solutions together.

The model of Jesus

In deciding how best to reveal himself as Saviour of the world, God could have chosen to establish a cutting edge website, rent a large stadium and arrange a live global satellite broadcast in multiple languages, as would perhaps have been suggested by some twenty-first century marketing experts had they been asked. But, instead, God chose a life as his strategy for reaching the world; a life that walked with people in the market place and played with children in the street; a life that rejoiced with people at their weddings and the birth of their children, then mourned with them at their funerals; a life that paid taxes and went to work as a fisherman; a life that was finite, that lived and died for us. It was that solitary life, Jesus, that ultimately changed the course of human history.[20]

If we think about that life of Jesus, we see that he spoke to people through stories and through personal relationship, through walking alongside people and sharing with them. Churches often rely on the youth or children's worker to deal with youth and family issues, but the church family is so much more than one worker. The Church also needs ordinary members of congregations who are willing to give time to build relationships with young people. These are people who see the value that children and young people bring as individuals and desire to walk, share and learn with them as they deal with the challenges and opportunities that life presents. By encouraging the development of a discipleship culture in our churches, with each person investing in the lives of a few others, many can be supported through all life's challenges, including those challenges within families. ■

18. Diana Butler Bass, *Christianity for the rest of us* (New York: HarperCollins, 2006), p.83

19. Alicia Britt Chole, *Purposeful proximity – Jesus' model of mentoring (2017)*
    http://enrichmentjournal.ag.org/200102/062_proximity.cfm [accessed 21 May 2017]

20. www.mentalhealth.org.uk/a-to-z/c/children-and-young-people

THINK

How are children and young people valued and supported within your congregation?

Would you respond differently to issues experienced by a family that attends church, and one that doesn't?

What does the life of Jesus teach us about building relationships with others?

READ

James R. Campbell, **Mentor like Jesus,** (Tennessee: B&H Publishing Group, 2009)

Alicia Britt Chole, **Purposeful proximity – Jesus' model of mentoring,** (2017) http://enrichmentjournal.ag.org/200102/062_proximity.cfm [accessed 21 May 2017]

Diana Butler Bass, **Christianity for the rest of us,** (New York: HarperCollins, 2006)

ACT

Identify a team of church members who will commit to building relationships with children and young people.

Do you always need to catch up with a neighbour or a friend over coffee after the church service? What about finding out what the children and young people have been doing or use a resource like 'Spill the Beans' to hold a catch-up session over coffee for a mixed age group.

Explore the opportunities for church members to undertake mentoring training.

RESOURCE

Spill the Beans www.spillbeans.org.uk

CPAS Mentoring matters www.cpas.org.uk/church-resources/mentoring-matters/#.WSWeUjOZNo4

YMCA Scotland Aspire mentoring www.ymcascotland.org/our-work/partnerships/#church-partnerships

DEALING WITH MENTAL HEALTH ISSUES

Stewart Cutler
Minister of St Ninian's Stonehouse Local Ecumenical Partnership

Everyone has mental health.

Each of us has a brain and the body systems that regulate how we feel. Each of us experiences emotions. We feel joy and sadness, anger and loss. When we are well we have the necessary resilience to manage our mood, to recognise when our mood doesn't match our situation, and to do things we know help make us feel better. When we can't do these things then we might have a problem with our mental health. It's no different to when things go wrong with our physical health. There are things we can all do to look after our wellbeing and there are things we should avoid. This is just as true for children and young people as it is for adults.

• Eating well – have fruit and healthy drinks instead of juice and biscuits

• Being active – get outside, play some games and run around. Sing!

• Being quiet – take time out to be still

• Paying attention – look out for each other and notice when things change or are not going well. Asking 'Are you okay?' can make all the difference.

Staying well is always the best place to start. Our wellbeing is actually at the heart of the Gospel. Jesus tells us not to worry (Matthew 6.25-34), which is easier said than done... But knowing that we are loved, that we can bring our concerns and worries to God in prayer, and that we belong to a community that cares for us are all hugely positive for our wellbeing.

Problems
The Mental Health Foundation suggests one in ten young people suffers from a mental health problem.[21] The most common conditions are depression, anxiety and self-harming. Other conditions include eating disorders and post-traumatic stress disorder. Some problems are related to changing hormones, puberty, bullying and body image.

The key to supporting children and young people with mental health problems is to be supportive. Say 'Hi!' when someone turns up; don't criticise them for not being along for a while. Don't pressure people into taking part. Pay attention. Listen. Don't leap to minimise how someone feels. Mental health problems often mean that someone can't just pull themselves together, even if they know they are unwell.

You might be the only person a child or young person may feel they can talk to. That's important. Your reaction could make all the difference so listen. You don't have to agree with the way someone presents themselves or the world, but try not to get into an argument or offer simple platitudes. Reassure.

21. https://www.mentalhealth.org.uk/a-to-z/c/children-and-young-people

Don't over reach. You're probably not a mental health nurse or a counsellor, so don't try to be one. If you think things are beyond your understanding or skills, then refer! That might best be done by building relationships with parents and passing concerns on to them, but try to keep information you have been given confidential and with teenagers seek their permission or encourage them to talk to their parents.

Like all safeguarding issues, if you believe that a child or young person is in danger then you must act to keep them safe. Suicide is the leading cause of death in young men in the UK. That's something we can all do something about. Asking someone if they have thought about taking their own life or if they have a plan will not encourage them to consider it. It may save their life.

Keeping good boundaries is also helpful. People with some conditions can be very needy and manipulative. You may want to be available to talk but do set limits on that. If it's a real crisis then encourage the young person to contact professional help. Keep a note of conversations, when they happen and what you talk about. You should also tell someone else you are supporting someone.

Training

Just like in the case of physical health, you can train in mental health awareness and first aid. Suicide awareness training is hugely worthwhile, especially if you work with teenagers. Contact your local association for mental health or Scottish Mental Health First Aid for dates.

What can churches do?

Talk about mental health. Create positive spaces where people can be open about how they feel and be supported when things are hard.

Promote anti-stigma work. Sign up to the See Me Movement For Change (https://www.seemescotland.org) and get involved.

Get to know each other better. We sometimes use our programmes to avoid having to get to know our children and young people. The opposite should be true; everything we do should be about building good relationships. Encourage people to be open and honest about how they feel. Create spaces in your programmes where you can all talk about how whatever you are exploring makes you feel. Developing language about emotions is hugely important.

What does the Bible say?

Not much – and lots. The Bible reflects how much our understanding of how our minds and bodies work has changed in 2,000 years. Many of the stories in the Gospels talk of demonic possession when describing what we might now term mental health problems. People were, and perhaps still are, afraid of people with severe mental health problems. Some conditions make people act in unpredictable ways. Some people may speak to themselves, hear voices or experience hallucinations. That can be distressing for them and for those around them. The last thing we should be doing is suggesting that mental health problems are the result of sin. We are called to be caring and understanding, to bring healing and compassion not condemnation. ∎

THINK

When do you feel down? When do you feel happy? Why?

How could you create a positive space for children and young people to talk about feelings?

How could you make sure there are activities that are quiet and reflective as well as active and noisy?

READ

Elament's young people section - www.elament.org.uk/young-people/

Young Minds - http://www.youngminds.org.uk

Mental Health and the Church: stories from NYA 2016 https://issuu.com/cofsyouth/docs/mental_health___the_church

Mark Yaconelli, Contemplative Youth Ministry – practicing the presence of Jesus, (London: SPCK, 2006)

ACT

Circle time – this can take a while. Sit in a circle, including the leaders. Ask a list of questions, some easy and some a bit deeper - like what is your favourite colour or what makes you feel sad or how do you feel about an issue or something that has happened. Depending on the age of the group you can vary your list of questions but don't be scared to ask about the deep stuff. Go round the circle with each question one at a time and each person answers the same question. Nobody is allowed to comment on any of the answers. At the end each person can ask one other person about one answer they gave. The idea is to encourage emotional literacy, to help people talk about their feelings.

RESOURCE

See Me - www.seemescotland.org

Young Minds - www.youngminds.org.uk

Young Scot's five ways to chill out in five minutes - http://youngscot.org/information/mind/5-ways-to-chill-out-in-5-minutes/

Mind and Soul Foundation - www.mindandsoulfoundation.org

Elament - www.elament.org.uk - self help tools, factsheets, contact details

My Story

Alastair Stark

Youth and Children's Worker

As a Youth and Children's worker, employed to work with five different congregations in Glenrothes and Leslie, the opportunities to engage with various teams around the town are both vast and extremely exciting. Between the five churches, there are examples of groups for primary school aged children, youth fellowships for those at secondary school, toddler groups and Messy Churches. We also work together to ensure there is chaplaincy provision for the twelve primary schools and three secondary schools across the parishes. Without the effort of successful teams in each of the churches, these groups would be impossible to sustain. A particular highlight for me though, is the way in which most of these churches run their annual summer holiday clubs.

The churches come together at a town-wide level to support each other in their holiday club provision. Each church has been called to serve in its own particular way and does this very well, but it is so exciting to see the way in which we come together. We share ideas, backdrops, props, fellowship and inspiration. We also pray for each other and take some time to reflect together.

Across the breadth of each local holiday club team, we naturally find those who are gifted in different areas. Some are ideally suited to a group leader role within a team and can take on the responsibility for a small group of children for the week. Others are more suited to the co-ordinator role, able to oversee the project and perhaps lead from the front

during the week too. We also need people with the gifts and skills to offer one to one support to particular children, to oversee the registration process, to organise refreshments, to promote the club in the local primary schools and to pray. Without a number of people with different gifts the teams would not be complete.

For me, one of the most exciting things is that each of the local holiday clubs has a faithful group of secondary school-aged volunteers. After all, the involvement of young people in leadership should be encouraged. Paul, in his letter to Timothy, writes: "Take the teachings that you heard me proclaim in the presence of many witnesses, and entrust them to reliable people, who will be able to teach others also" (2 Timothy 2.2).

I firmly believe that holiday clubs such as these should be celebrated, as they encourage us to work together in a way that opens up possibilities within our own congregations, with other congregations and with, not just for, our children and young people.

God has called and equipped each of us to be involved in youth and children's ministry, even if we may not currently realise it. Whether our strengths involve jumping around and leading from the front, or bringing out the juice and biscuits, or being a prayer warrior, we all have something special to give. ∎

My Story

Julie Saunders

Volunteer with the GK Experience

At the time of writing this I have been volunteering with the GK Experience for almost a year. My story of joining the team is a strange one, but very meaningful. I am from the USA and came to Scotland in September 2015 as a volunteer through a partnership program between the Presbyterian Church USA and the Church of Scotland Priority Areas. Four other American volunteers and I were placed in different Priority Area parishes around Glasgow. I was in Gorbals Parish Church working in the Café, and with other charities linked to the church. I came into contact with The GK Experience when they held their AGM at Gorbals Parish Church where I happened to be working. I was able to hear about all the wonderful work they do with young people and couldn't resist getting involved. I started spending my one day off, a Monday, at the GK office helping out where I could.

I never imagined how much I would grow to love the people involved in the organisation, and the young people they work with. I started off doing odd but important tasks like sorting kit and making tea and soon grew to having more responsibilities. The GK office is a mad, busy, and thriving place. In the office there are the regular staff members, as well as many volunteers popping in and out each day. Some of my best memories come from working in the GK office planning for residential events or training days. With many volunteers working together it can be difficult because of the many personalities helping to run the different pieces of work. We have to be understanding of each other and adaptable to be able to get the pieces of work done together, but we also have fun while we are doing it.

We very much operate as a team caring for each other while working together; the practical tasks like logistics for a local club and personal tasks like celebrating birthdays or passing an exam are considered equally important. The saying in Glasgow is "People Make Glasgow" and I would also attribute this saying to the GK Experience. Being so far from family the GK Experience has been a home away from home for me. I value the hard work that GK does and they go above and beyond to make everyone involved in the organisation feel a part of a big family. They value their volunteers both at work and in their personal lives.

Working in the office I notice the small acts of kindness they do for people in the organisation, whether it is a birthday card, a celebratory bouquet of flowers, or just a cup of tea and a chat when someone is having a life crisis. I myself have felt this love and kindness many times even in my small amount of time volunteering with them. I am so thankful to the GK Experience for welcoming me into the family, challenging me to be the best version of myself, and changing my life through the work they do as an organisation. ■

FORMING TOGETHER

MISSION AND/OR DISCIPLESHIP

Graeme McMeekin
Head of Church Development, Tearfund Scotland

One of the debates that rumble among Christians who work with children and young people is the question of 'Youth/Children's Ministry' and 'Christian Youth/Children's work'. The terms themselves are not particularly useful as both involve work and ministry, but the interpretation of the terms and what they mean in practice can be considered distinct. Youth/Children's Ministry is commonly understood to have an emphasis on discipleship. Based upon the description of the earliest church after Pentecost, where "they were devoting themselves to the apostle's teaching and to fellowship, to the breaking of bread and to prayer" (Acts 2.42), this ministry involves Christian teaching, fellowship, worship and prayer. In other words, the work itself is distinctly Christian in its content and normally aimed at those who already have an active connection with the Church. Pete Ward describes this as the Inside-Out model.[22]

Christian Youth/Children's Work differs in the sense that the focus is not on delivering Christian content to those within the Church. Motivated by their faith, those involved in Christian Youth/Children's work focus on reaching beyond the boundaries of the Church, often to those who have no church connection, and may or may not explicitly involve Christian content. This work may be described as having an emphasis on mission, and sometimes explicitly has the aim of evangelism, while in other cases has a much broader agenda. Ward describes this as the Outside-In model.

What is mission?

In the corporate world, companies may talk about their 'Mission Statement', which is simply a punchy statement that outlines what they intend to achieve as a company. For the Church, however, the understanding of mission has primarily focused on the root of the word which means 'to send'.

In 1910, during the era of colonialism, the World Missionary Conference met in Edinburgh and focused on taking the gospel to unreached people groups overseas, teaching them about Christ and planting Churches. If we use this as a model of mission in youth and children's work, then our focus may be on evangelism, taking every opportunity to tell an unreached generation about Jesus and, like the pioneers of colonisation, pray that this will result in both spiritual and behavioural change.

Since the Second World War and the process of decolonisation, however there has been an emphasis on the doctrine of *missio Dei* (Mission of God). Drawing from John 17, David Bosch explains that as well as God the Father sending the Son, and God the Father and the Son sending the Spirit, we also have God the Father, Son, and Holy Spirit sending the church into the world.[23]

In light of this, our mission is to participate as God's people in God's own mission for the redemption of God's creation, at God's invitation and command.[24] Therefore, drawing on Romans 8.18-25, those who endorse the *missio Dei* principle perceive the created world and its social relationships as broken or decaying and awaiting God's reparation. In light of this, the Church has a role in being a sign of what God is doing and is going to do. For the Christian Youth/Children's worker, this often means enabling and empowering young people/children not only to challenge injustice in the world, but also to equip them to thrive by providing them with opportunities that they may not otherwise have.

What is discipleship?

For those involved in Youth/Children's ministry, Matthew 28.19-20 provides a particular motivation for their work:

"Therefore go and make disciples of all nations, baptizing them in the name of the Father and the Son and the Holy Spirit, teaching them to obey everything I have commanded you. And remember, I am with you always, to the end of the age." Matthew 28.19-20

The word mathētēs, which we translate as 'disciples', is better translated as 'learners', therefore we may read Jesus' commission as "go and make learners of all nations ...". However the question remains about how and what we are expecting them to learn. Sylvia Wilkey Collinson has undertaken an extensive study on discipleship in the New Testament, and notes that discipleship is normally intentional, does not follow a set curriculum, and involves learning from each other in such a way that at times the learners are the teachers, according to their own expertise.[25] Therefore, discipleship in the context of youth/children's ministry should not be about the adult teaching children/young people, but rather about creating opportunities for learning together with the adult being as much a disciple learning from those they seek to serve.

Mission without discipleship and vice versa

There can be no doubt that mission and discipleship are distinct from each other[26], yet they are intrinsically linked with many similarities. Both involve the children/young people learning and going through a process of transformation or conversion, either in the sense of a transformation of how they relate to the world or in how they become more distinctly Christian. Nonetheless, mission without discipleship results in a lack of understanding in the Christian faith that has motivated the work in the first place. Likewise discipleship without mission lacks purpose and focus resulting in a ministry that has the potential to isolate and not fully equip the person for Christian living. As a Church we cannot just focus on one, mission or discipleship; instead we are called to both. ∎

22. Pete Ward, *Youthwork and the Mission of God*, (London: SPCK, 1997), p.7

23. David Bosch, *Transforming Mission: Paradigm shifts in theology of mission*, (Marynoll, NY: Orbis, 1991), p.309

24. Christopher JH. Wright, *The Mission of God: Unlocking the Bible's grand narrative*, (Nottingham: IVP, 2006), p.23

25. Sylvia W. Collinson, *Making Disciples: The significance of Jesus' Educational Methods for Today's Church*, (Milton Keynes: Paternoster, 2004), p.23

26. As described in Naomi Stanton, *Faith-based Youth Work – Lessons from the Christian sector*, in Sheila Curran et al., *Working with Young People* (2nd ed.), (London: Sage, 2013)

THINK

Does each person need to be involved in both discipleship and mission or can they focus on one and have other aspects of the Church focus on the other?

What can our children/young people teach us about the Christian faith?

Does discipleship need to happen with in the Church or are there other contexts in which this can happen?

READ

Sylvia W. Collinson, **Making Disciples: The significance of Jesus' Educational Methods for Today's Church,** (Milton Keynes: Paternoster, 2004)

Maxine Green, **Youth Worker as Converter,** in Sarah Banks (ed.), **Ethical Issues in Youth Work** (2nd edition), (London: Routledge, 2010), pp.123-137

Mark K. Smith et al., **Youth Work and Faith: Debates, Delights and Dilemmas,** (Lyme Regis: Russell House, 2015)

Pete Ward, **Youthwork and the Mission of God** Christopher JH. Wright, **The Mission of God: Unlocking the Bible's grand narrative,** (Nottingham: IVP, 2006)

ACT

Schedule a session in which the young people or children teach the adults about the challenges of living as a Christian young person today, ensuring that you allow them time to prepare.

Create a forum in your church where you can ask the children/young people involved about the barriers for their friends coming in? This may be a painful exercise as they may indicate areas for change.

Read through the book of Acts and note down each time someone is missional, and how this was done.

RESOURCE

Table Talk – this is a series of board games and mobile applications with questions that can be answered by leaders and young people/children on an equal footing. They open up discussion on a range of pertinent and mundane issue

Energize - this resource has been developed by Urban Saints in order to be used for both outreach and mission.

Conferences and Training Events – these provide a useful forum to listen to others and to find out what others are doing at any given time.

FAITH FORMATION

Ewen Glen
Youth and Family Development Worker for Lothian Presbytery

Whether we serve the children, young people and their families of our church by cooking, leading clubs, preaching or through personal prayer, together we are working towards the same goal. We wish to see children and young people form life-long faith in Jesus Christ. There are many experiences we all go through as we come to and develop our faith and as a result there is no fail-safe programme or magic pill. We are becoming increasingly aware of the challenges facing the Church of Scotland in developing the next generation of life-long disciples of Christ. The numbers of children and young people engaging in church are decreasing and increasingly few are finding faith in later adult life.

Challenge

In hoping to reverse this trend we perhaps need to learn from the testimony of those like Peter, the disciple of Jesus, who, despite ups and downs, pursued life-long faith in Christ Jesus. Peter's faith journey starts in his natural environment by Lake Galilee. In Luke 5.1-11 we find him listening to the teaching of Jesus, who has commissioned his fishing boat as a culturally appropriate soap box. We are not told the content of what Jesus is teaching, rather the narrative records in detail what happened next. Jesus issues Peter a challenge. "Put out into deep water, and let down the nets for a catch" (Luke 5.4). Peter took up the challenge and discovered that all he thought he knew and believed about fishing had to be rewritten now Jesus was in his boat.

It was this experience of Peter responding to the challenge of faith issued by Jesus that led him to confess and trust in Jesus as Lord. It wasn't the teaching of Jesus alone that led Peter to faith but the challenge to trust him in a matter of everyday life. In recent years our discipleship of children and young people has often focused on traditional classroom style learning (ever wondered why we call it Sunday School!?). But sadly the learning rarely leaves the classroom to be applied in everyday life.

To encourage faith formation we must no longer see children and young people as simply empty vessels to be filled with knowledge but rather as fellow pilgrims on a journey as we trust Jesus together. This also means we must free them from the classroom in order to live lives of faith in and among the church community.

Our role in the faith formation of children and young people is to challenge, encourage, and equip them as they grow and mature as life-long disciples of Jesus.

Experience

When Jesus hears Peter's confession of sin he doesn't sign him up to a twelve-week course on repentance and recovery. Rather, he gives him a new role and responsibility - "from now on you will fish for people" (Luke 5.10).

Some might say Peter has too underdeveloped a faith (or even a childlike faith) for the role of evangelist. Those same voices would urge against giving children roles to play in the church before they reach a more mature understanding. Yet Peter's faith doesn't develop in the classroom but side by side with Jesus on the road as he experiences daily what it means to serve, trust and even fail him.

As we wish faith to form and develop in our children and young people we need to create spaces and opportunities that allow them, like Peter, to experience faith and be challenged by it. We need to enable them to pray rather than always praying for them. We need to enable them to be involved in creating times of worship and the spaces in which worship occurs. We need to enable them to read the Bible and ask questions of it themselves. We need to enable them to serve rather than doing everything for them. We need to enable them to grapple with the big questions of life rather than shielding them from tough topics or only giving them easy answers.

Expressions of faith development

The theologian John Westerhoff III understands faith as a development of expressions.[27] The first expression of faith, often experienced in childhood, is in the form of interactions with others. Children learn to express faith as they witness the faith of their family and community.

As children grow into early adulthood they begin to transition into a new stage as their faith becomes characterised by critical thinking. More than ever questions demand an answer, one that addresses their ever expanding life experiences.

Having moved through those stages faith may now grow towards maturity, no longer dependent on affiliation to the faith of the family or a particular community but convicted of a personal allegiance to God, and as a result able to better serve others in the formation of their faith.

In each of these expressions the whole faith community is essential for the development of faith. We see this particularly when a child or young person's faith transitions between the first couple of expressions. During this transition they may begin to rebel against an affiliation to their parents or church community. They may experiment with lifestyles or beliefs contrary to Christian teaching. This is not the time to panic! Instead, this is the time to make the most of the investment the church community has made in their childhood - to encourage an openness to engage with difficult questions and issues so that they might know you are committed to their wellbeing.

Our role in the faith formation of children and young people is to challenge, encourage, and equip them as they grow and mature as life-long disciples of Jesus. ■

27. John H. Westerhoff, *Bringing Up Children in the Christian Faith*, (Minneapolis: Winston Press, Inc., 1980), p.32

THINK

How might you challenge your children and young people to put teaching into practice?

What experiences were transformational in your own faith development? How could you the children and young people in your congregation?

Should a young person/family stop attending your church how would you demonstrate your continued commitment to them?

READ

John H. Westerhoff III, **Will Our Children Have Faith?,** (New York: Morehouse Publishing, 3rd Revised Edition, 2012)

Nick Shepherd, **Faith Generation,** (London: SPCK, 2016)

Kenda Creasy Dean, **Almost Christian: what the faith of our teenagers is telling the American church,** (Oxford: Oxford University Press, 2010)

Kara E. Powell, Brad M. Griffin, and Cheryl Crawford, **Sticky Faith Youth Worker Edition: practical ideas to nurture long-term faith in teenagers,** (Grand Rapids: Zondervan, 2011)

ACT

Transitions of faith expression often coincide with transitions in life experience such as moving from primary school into secondary school. When a child is due to move to a new school the church could show its support by praying over the child and their family. On the first day of school you could provide them with a school survival kit including new stationery, notebooks and a calculator along with a written prayer or letter of encouragement.

RESOURCE

Faith in homes - http://www.faithinhomes.org.uk/

Kara E. Powell, **The Sticky Faith Guide for Your Family: Over 100 practical and tested ideas to build lasting faith in kids,** (Grand Rapids: Zondervan, 2014)

Martyn Payne and Jane Butcher, **The Barnabas Family Bible: 110 Bible stories for families to share,** (Abingdon: The Bible Reading Fellowship, 2014)

PARTICIPATION

Jonathon Fraser
Youth Minister for Hilton Parish Church

A cultural shift has taken place. While those born in the early 1990s and before will gladly go to the cinema to be entertained, today's youth are not nearly so content to sit passively in rows, watching the action unfold before them (which sounds much like Church). The advent of YouTube demonstrates that today's adolescents want to be in their own movies; active participants, part of the story.

Participatory knowledge

This is a shift towards 'participatory knowledge.' Think of it like learning a language. There are educational models (e.g. learning grammar, memorising vocabulary, listening to recordings), then there are participatory (or immersive) models. In the Gaelic School in Inverness for example, pupils - whether they know the language or not - are spoken to in Gaelic from their first day onwards. By participating in an environment where Gaelic is the only language used, it is learned remarkably quickly. This is not to say one cannot learn a language through different models, but to emphasise the particular strength and effectiveness of participatory knowledge. Participatory knowledge marks the qualitative difference between knowing about something and knowing something.

Putting this in terms of faith, Luther and the Reformers distinguished between two ways of believing. We can believe certain things about God, for example that God exists and that Jesus lived and died, but rather than having true faith, this form of belief is simply having knowledge about God. To believe in

We need to recognise that children and young people are not a demographic.

God and thereby not only to have knowledge about God but also to put trust in God, surrendering to God, is to know God.[28] By participating in worship, therefore, we do not acquire knowledge about Jesus; we come to know Jesus.

All of this tells us that today's children and young people are more interested in participatory knowledge than in educational processes. Unfortunately, within the Church of Scotland, we have worked almost exclusively using educational models (Sunday School, Bible Class, Communicants Course). While not denying the importance of education, developing youth and children's ministry in the twenty-first century will need Churches to foster an openness that enables children and young people to enter into the mystery of worship and the presence of God.

The priesthood of all believers

Perhaps surprisingly, a rediscovery of the Protestant doctrine of the priesthood of all believers might prove helpful. Rather than providing any 'how to' models, I hope to utilise this doctrine to argue that participation in the priestly office - that belongs to all who are in Christ - is absolutely necessary for the proper functioning of youth and children's ministry and, indeed, the Church as a whole.

The Roman Catholic hierarchy of priests in the sixteenth century prompted Luther to assert that 'we are all priests before God if we are Christians.[29] In the early Protestant Churches, the priesthood of all believers was a lived reality - and they meant all believers, regardless of age. For example, when in Geneva Calvin stressed that all are one in Christ Jesus (Galatians 3.28), he meant that there was an equality of believers, an equality of ministers and an equality of ministers and believers.[30]

That all God's people are priests is a truth testified throughout Scripture (c.f. Exodus 19.6; 1 Peter 2.5-9; Revelation 1.6, 5.10, 20.6). But what does it mean to say all God's people are priests? Luther explained that just as we are not called Christians because of our wealth but because of our faith in Christ, so too we are not called priests because of the priestly clothing we wear but because we come into God's presence.[31]

Likewise, Calvin understood all Christian believers to have immediate and personal access to God the Father through Christ, and so all could be described as priests.[32] As the Levitical priests of the Old Testament came near to God and ministered before him (Ezekiel 43.19), so in the New Testament all believers are permitted access to the presence of God through Christ's sacrifice (Hebrews 10.19-20).

Participation in practice

Participation in the priestly office is transformative and life-changing because it means access to the transformative and life-changing presence of God. The problem in many of our congregations today is that we are not enabling our children and young people to participate as priests, but are relying on the participation of us as adults in the practices of the church on their behalf. The activities we run for our children and young people often don't engage them in mission in their own right, lacking as they do any participation in acts that provoke faith and produce wonder.[33]

So, rather than confining children and young people to certain pews or sequestering them in the church hall, we need to make opportunities for them to fully participate in the priestly office that is as much theirs in Christ as it is ours. We need to recognise that children and young people are not a demographic that we minister to, but priests of God we minster with. Therefore, we need to make sure that they are active participants in all the practices that lead us into the presence of God - our discipleship-making, our hospitality, our proclamation, our serving and our worship.

We have been chosen by God to share in Christ's own royal priesthood. This is as true for young believers as it is for adults. The challenge for the Church, then, is to create a culture in which every believer understands they are a priest of God and part of a holy priesthood (1 Peter 2.5) and to create opportunities for young and old alike to participate in the mystery of God's presence in our midst. ∎

THINK

Where are the children and young people in your church? Are they there at all? Are they on the periphery? Are they central to who you are as God's people in your particular time and place?

What objections exist in your context (if any) to the full participation of young people in the practices of your church?

Have you ever given much thought to the doctrine of the priesthood of all believers? How might this change your understanding of the role of children and youth in your fellowship?

READ

Anizor, Uche and Voss, Hank, **Representing Christ: A Vision for the Priesthood of All Believers,** (Downers Grove: InterVarsity Press, 2016)

Sylvia Collins-Mayo, Bob Mayo, Sally Nash and Christopher Cocksworth, **The Faith of Generation Y,** (London: Church House Publishing, 2010)

Kenda C. Dean, and Ron Foster, **The Godbearing Life: the art of soul tending for youth ministry,** (Nashville: Upper Room Books, 2005)

Mark DeVries, **Focusing Youth Ministry through the Family in eds.** Kenda C. Dean, Chap Clark and Dave Rhan, **Starting Right: Thinking Theologically about Youth Ministry,** (Grand Rapids: Zondervan, 2001)

Majorie J. Thompson, **Soul Feast: An Invitation to the Christian Spiritual Life,** (Louisville: Westminster John Knox Press, 1995)

ACT

Reflect together on Mark 10.13-16. What would it look like to make children and young people as central to the life and witness of your church as they are to the kingdom of God?

Do some 'every-member' ministry: minister to the poor together, practice hospitality across the generations, give a young person an opportunity to preach, let your youth serve you communion.

RESOURCE

Perhaps the greatest resource is the children and young people in your congregation

Voice activated: Developing participation in the Methodist Church www.methodist.org.uk/media/1466864/voice-activated-whole-document.pdf

28. Daniel L. Migliore, *Faith Seeking Understanding*, (Cambridge: Wm. B. Eerdmans, 2004), p.236

29. He quotes Martin Luther, *A Brief Explanation of the Ten Commandments, the Creed, and the Lord's Prayer*

30. Martin Luther, *The Epistles of St. Peter and St. Jude, trans. EH. Gillet,* (New York: Anson D.F. Randolph, 1859), p.106

31. John R. Crawford, *Calvin and the Priesthood of All Believers* in The Scottish Journal of Theology vol. 21, issue 2 (1968), pp. 145-156

32. Luther, *The Epistles of St. Peter and St. Jude*, p.107

33. Crawford, *Calvin and the Priesthood of All Believers*, p.146

QUESTIONING

Richard Knott
Children's and Youth Development Worker for the United Free Church of Scotland

One Sunday a minister was using squirrels as part of an object lesson with the children. He started, "I'm going to describe something, and I want you to raise your hand when you know what it is." The children nodded eagerly. "This thing lives in trees (pause) and eats nuts (pause)…" No hands went up. "It is grey (pause) and has a long bushy tail (pause)…" The children were looking at each other nervously, but still no hands rose. "It jumps from branch to branch (pause) and chatters and flips its tail when it's excited (pause)…" Finally one little boy tentatively raised his hand. The pastor quickly called on him. "Well," said the boy, "I know the answer must be "Jesus" … but it sure sounds like a squirrel!"

You have probably heard that one before. It is an old joke, but its underlying message still has a certain ring of truth! The questions that we ask children are often in this vain; they are questions that we don't expect the children to think very much about, where the answer is obvious and it is almost always Jesus!

Knowing the answers

The questions we ask are often simply a tactic for seeking the regurgitation of the facts of the Biblical narrative we have just read or heard. Questions such as who said what? Who then did what? How many this or that were there? In today's culture of 'alternative facts' I am not suggesting that Biblical facts are unimportant, but I would suggest that perhaps they are not the most important things to focus our questions on.   In truth, these questions are likely to be for the benefit of the leaders rather than the children. Receiving the correct responses enables us to check and assess that the children have 'got the story' and can remember it; if they can, we feel satisfied that we have done our job.

It is important to remember that a living faith in Jesus is not achieved by being able to recite verses of Scripture or by knowing all the facts. Consider, for example, when Jesus was tempted in the wilderness. Satan used facts and texts from Scripture to tempt Jesus and would therefore likely know all the answers to our Bible quizzes. So I would like to suggest an alternative approach - one where the search for meaning is not always found in this type of regurgitation of the facts. The type of search for meaning that finds a connection with our own experience and leads to a transformation in our lives is a more fulfilling and ambitious goal than that of simply remembering key facts.

Opening up questions

In general terms there are two types of questions - open and closed. The type we have referred to so far are the closed questions; those with black and white, right or wrong answers. Closed questions close down discussion; once the right answer has been given to the questioner's satisfaction the topic is then closed. Open questions on the other hand are those to which a variety of responses exist; rather than black or white, right or wrong answers there are many shades of grey. These questions allow children and young people to share differing and perhaps even opposing ideas and to benefit from a range of viewpoints as they wrestle for themselves with the issue in hand.

❝ The danger with simply filling silences with more questions or explanations is that we discourage children and young people from engaging deeply.

Wondering

One methodology that exemplifies this approach is Godly Play which uses what it calls 'wondering' as a way to help participants explore and find meaning for themselves. This style of questioning asks participants to share their thoughts on the story and issues at hand by asking person centred questions such as, I wonder what you liked in this story? I wonder what the most important part of the story is? These are questions that only an individual can answer for themselves so importantly there are no right or wrong answers and everyone's views and responses are valid and equally valued. This way of wondering and discussing together can go on for some time as individuals explore many possible and potential meanings.

The goal behind such a wondering approach is to provide children and young people with opportunities to explore what they think and feel as they listen to God for themselves, rather than aiming to arrive at the conclusion planned in advance by the adult leading the session. Not putting a specific end point in place can be unsettling for those leading the session but it gives the Spirit more freedom to move, often in mysterious and unexpected ways.

Auditory space

It is not just a case of asking the right questions; sensitivity is also required in gauging the heartfelt nature or otherwise of responses. Perhaps sometimes we think it is our job to speak and to fill silences rather than to create spaces for discovery and have the patience it might take to really listen to children and young people. Dr Rebecca Nye refers to 'auditory space' and encourages us to talk less and listen more. She suggests internally counting to at least seven when at first no one responds to an open question to give the time needed to reflect and consider a response fully before it is shared.[34]

The danger with simply filling silences with more questions or explanations is that we discourage children and young people from engaging deeply. While it can be difficult to train ourselves to operate in such a way, it is worth showing our response and interest in what our children and young people are thinking and sharing through facial expressions and 'mmms' rather than prematurely intruding into their auditory space. By doing this we show that all responses have value; we value their thoughts so are giving them time to think and respond. This in turn will encourage others in the group to also offer their own responses and everyone benefits from the questioning and wondering that takes place. ■

34. Rebecca Nye, *Children's spirituality: what it is and why it matters*, (London: Church House Publishing, 2009), p.45

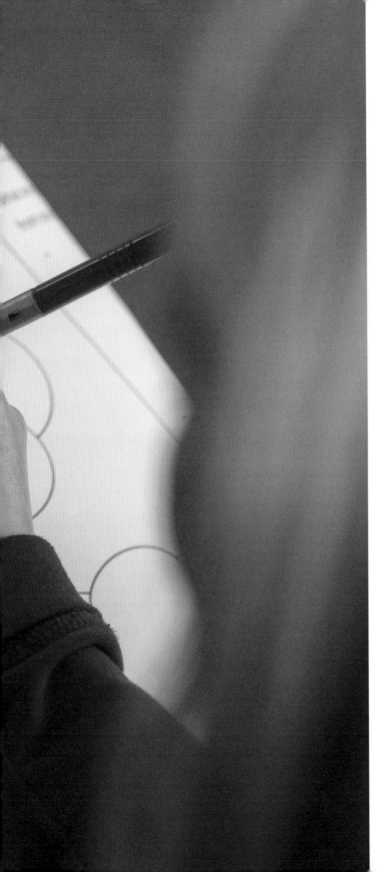

THINK

I wonder how the idea of not seeking a right or wrong answer makes you feel.

I wonder if you feel better knowing that you are not expected to know all the answers.

I wonder how comfortable you feel in the role of a guide, exploring deep questions alongside children and young people.

I wonder what you have learnt from the children and young people as you shared the Biblical narrative with them.

READ

Rebecca Nye, **Children's Spirituality: what it is and why it matters,** (London: Church House Publishing, 2009)

Jerome W. Berryman, **Teaching Godly Play: how to mentor the spiritual development of children,** (Denver: Moorhouse Education Resources, 2009)

ACT

Perhaps you could try to create a safe space for children and young people to respond to open 'wondering' questions remembering to give time for responses to be formulated. It may take a little time and encouragement for the group and leaders to get used to the idea that there is not one correct answer.

RESOURCE

Godly Play Scotland www.godlyplayscotland.co.uk/

Jim Candy, Brad M. Griffin and Kara Powell, **Can I Ask That: 8 hard questions about God and Faith, a Sticky Faith Curriculum,** (Pasadena: Fuller Youth Institute, 2014)

Table Talk www.theuglyducklingcompany.com/Table-talk.html

Discipleship Deck www.fusionmovement.org/resources/product/14

CHILDREN, YOUNG PEOPLE AND JUSTICE

Fiona Buchanan

Youth Development Officer, Christian Aid Scotland

The Christian Aid Collective is a movement of young people desperate to create a different world - a world without poverty and injustice, a world where everyone has what they need to live life in all its fullness. This is driven by our belief in a God who created a world in which every single person on the planet is loved and infinitely valued. We believe that the way the world is today – a world in which millions of people go to bed hungry every night, a world in which nearly a billion people live in extreme poverty, and a world that is controlled by structures that oppress people for their gender, race or sexuality – is not the world that God intended.

We want to create a space where young people can grow to know a God who radically loves the poor and to empower them to follow the pattern of the early Church which built a community where everyone's needs were met.

What we do?

The Christian Aid Collective is building a movement of young people who want to globally tackle poverty and to challenge structures that keep people poor.

We believe that God created a world that was meant to be connected – people, planet and God existing together in good relationships. The Christian Aid Collective exists to connect young people to the world around them, to the people and communities around them, and to a God who cares radically for the poor.

We exist to:
- Connect young people to other people around the world who are affected by the structures that are keeping people poor.

- Empower young people to use their voices to speak out against injustice, to act prophetically to challenge systems and structures that maintain a world that is not as God intended, and to build community locally and globally that ensures everyone's needs are met.

- Provide an ecumenical platform for young people to share the ways that their church traditions and faiths meet a God who cares for the poor.

What is Christian Aid Collective theology?

Christian Aid was set up by a collection of churches in 1945 and today has forty-six supporting church denominations who come alongside us to see God's vision for justice and peace realised in the world.

Because of this the Christian Aid Collective exists to help a wide range of church traditions explore what it means to meet a God who cares for the poor within their specific theologies. We provide a platform for young people of varying traditions to share their opinions and engage in dialogue about how their faith drives them to work for a better world.

The Collective's theology is shaped around a vision inspired by the early church and their model of community as a way to exist together in a better world. We believe in a thread of justice and equality throughout the Bible and our work is rooted in our belief in a God of liberation who repeatedly hears the cry of the oppressed and acts to bring freedom and restore relationships.

Storytelling

The world is broken, but we believe we were made for more than this. We can bring about a better world when we connect to our neighbours and exist in community. For the Collective one of the most effective ways of achieving this is through storytelling. We are bound together by our stories, so when poverty and injustice impact anyone, anywhere, it's a threat to everyone, everywhere. Not only does the sharing of stories enable us to build community and connect to our global neighbours, it enables us to inspire and engage with children and young people here in Scotland on issues of justice. Through storytelling we want to inspire people to act, to campaign, to share stories, to pray, to give, to fundraise and to build community. ∎

Janeh

This is Janeh - she's a twenty-three year old student... and a refugee.

She was a student of English literature at Damascus University. Then the conflict started. She would lie awake at night listening to the sound of bombs around the city. It became too dangerous so she and her family fled to Iraq. For some people a war might, understandably, have diminished their hopes, but not for Janeh. She has now been accepted to study fine art at a local university. She spends the rest of her time running workshops for children to help with the psychological impact of war.

Madj

This is Madj - he's a skin doctor...and a refugee.

He worked hard in Syria: he had a highly qualified job, a car and money in the bank. When we met him he had gone from that lifestyle to selling shoes by the side of the road. He decided to leave Syria as it was too dangerous. He's been making his way to Germany laden with bags of his belongings. He is unable to access his money so, for now, he is trapped in this way of life. He feels angry that people think refugees are coming to Europe just for money and work, as his life in Syria – in his homeland - was better. His story shows that war doesn't discriminate by economic standards; it ruins and disrupts everyone's lives.

THINK

How can you connect young people in your community with those from around the world?

What are your reflections on the 'thread of justice' running through the Bible?

How can the telling of stories help you to build community and challenge injustice in your own context? What is your story?

READ

Read more about Christian Aid's work www.christianaid.org.uk

Read more stories gathered by the Christian Aid Collective www.christianaidcollective.org/

ACT

Why not get your children and young people involved in Christian Aid's campaigns www.christianaidcollective.org/do/campaign

Follow the Collective on Instagram and share your stories with us www.instagram.com/thecacollective/

We send a monthly text message with a campaign action or a film to share. It's totally free; text JOIN to 70060.

RESOURCE

Christian Aid Collective Bible studies
www.christianaidcollective.org/do/bible-studies

Do Not Tiptoe, the Christian Aid Collective's magazine exploring issues of injustice, poverty, theology, storytelling and community
www.christianaidcollective.org/do/magazine

Christian Aid Collective films online
www.christianaidcollective.org/do/film
and www.christianaidcollective.org/eat-act-pray

Christian Aid resources for children
www.christianaid.org.uk/resources/churches/resources/
children-in-church.aspx

CHILDREN, YOUNG PEOPLE AND THE WORLD

Val Brown
Church and Community Manager, Christian Aid Scotland and Vice Convenor of the World Mission Council

Listening to Churches around the world

The World Mission Council of the Church of Scotland is privileged to hear the voices of our partner Churches from right around the world, and walk alongside them in our common journey of faith. We are able to hear the joys, the sorrows, the hopes, the frustrations and the challenges that our partners face being the Church in their context. We often have much to learn from the global Church as we can be inspired by their vision, their passion and their energy for the gospel. We often are given food for thought as we hear how people cope and deal with experiences of violence, conflict and oppression, or of crops lost as climate change takes hold.

Our partner Churches across Africa and the Caribbean shared with us how climate change is making it harder and harder for people to grow crops successfully. Many of the churches we link with are made up of people in rural areas who rely on the land for their livelihoods. It is important for the churches in these places to be in the front-line of combatting climate change, educating farmers and campaigning for change, including telling us, their global partners, what we can do to support them.

One example is in Sumba, a small Island in the Indonesian archipelago, where our partner church is at the forefront of campaigning to protect the forests and natural environment as congregation members rely on the land to exist.

Called to action

If we take seriously our belief that 'we are all part of the one body', then it is not enough for us to merely hear these voices and ignore them; rather, they must compel us to act standing in solidarity with our sisters and brothers who are struggling. Often this means that we have to examine our own priorities, our own theology and our own actions.

Christian Aid has been working on climate change since 2007, as their partners from right around the world were telling them they had to. The message that came to Christian Aid from a partner in Bangladesh was, "forget about making poverty history. Climate change will make poverty permanent".[35] If people can't make their land productive then they will

leave it. It is often young people who bear the brunt of this, losing out on their education or being forced to migrate to look for work, often ending up in the slums of large cities.

Hearing the voices of our partner churches forces us to think about our theology – what do we think about climate change, energy sources, consumerism, high carbon life-styles, and how do we relate that to our faith in Jesus Christ? Christian Aid's work on climate change, alongside the voices of our own partner churches, has informed the work of the Church and Society Council of the Church of Scotland, the part of the Church that speaks on policy and engages with the Government. Recently the Council worked alongside eco-congregations to take a baton to Paris ahead of the climate change talks, asking that world leaders would commit to changes that would curb carbon emissions, and at the 2016 General Assembly the Council asked the Church to consider divesting from fossil fuels; a conversation that is on-going.

In Syria, our partner Church has become a front-line humanitarian aid organisation, because it has had to. The devastating conflict in that land has left people displaced, hungry and in need of emergency supplies. Through the Church of Scotland's 'place at the table' appeal, congregations and individuals are able to stand with our partner church and support the relief they are giving to all people, regardless of their faith. In Egypt, we have appointed a new mission partner to support the work of the Protestant Church there, and he gives some of his time to the work that St Andrew's United Church in Cairo does in offering much needed support to refugees. Part of the work ensures that children are able to access education, as well psycho-social support.

Engaging in difficult questions

And in the "Holy Land", the Church of Scotland has a historic presence – we have two Churches, a guesthouse, a hotel and a school. We hear the cry of the Palestinian Christians, many of whom are living under occupation in the West Bank, asking for us to help them get their freedom back. That poses hard questions for us as a Church here that we need to grapple

35. *A Fairer, Brighter Future. Why we should take action on climate change, (2014)* Christian Aid, http://www.christianaid.org.uk/Images/A-fairer-brighter-future-June-2014.pdf [accessed September 2016]

with intelligently and responsibly. How do we read the Bible through the eyes of those that are weakest and most marginalised and challenge theologies that don't uphold the dignity and worth of all individuals? How do we use our presence in that land to bring about a just peace for all people who call it home?

As we journey with the global church and our global Christian Aid partners, we need to be prepared to be challenged, to speak out, to change ourselves and our practices so that as a Church here in Scotland we can play an active part in living out the Biblical imperatives for justice and the very clear gospel bias to the poor. As we work alongside children and young people here, we need to think about how we communicate faith, how we allow space for them to learn about the global church, and perhaps most crucially, how we enable them to equate their faith with what they are learning in the classroom and the world they are seeing around them. To have an active, living faith, it has to be relevant to the questions, challenges and possibilities of today. Having global issues, stories and actions embedded into youth and children's ministry is an important way to enable this. ■

To have an active, living faith, it has to be relevant to the questions, challenges and possibilities of today.

THINK

What global issues does your youth work currently address?

Is there a reason that you haven't engaged in more global issues?

What opportunities would a global perspective bring to what you are currently doing?

READ

Christian Aid's policy reports and theological papers
www.christianaid.org.uk/resources/churches/what-we-believe.aspx

The World Mission Council reports
www.churchofscotland.org.uk/serve/world_mission/reports_and
_resources

ACT

Consider sending your young adults to the Church of Scotland National Youth Assembly where global issues are often discussed and then allow them space to offer feedback on what they have learned

Encourage your children and young people to get involved in the World Mission Council's Souper Sunday and/or a 'twinning'

Work with your local schools bringing a faith perspective to world issues

Invite a speaker from Christian Aid or the World Mission Council to speak to your groups about particular issues

RESOURCE

Christian Aid and Tearfund have resources to be used in schools, children's groups and youth groups

Messy Church have resources to run a God's Worldwide Family session

The World Mission Council have a world themed holiday club –
Professor Potty's Time Traveller's Tales

FRESH EXPRESSIONS OF CHURCH WITH CHILDREN AND YOUNG PEOPLE

Martyn Payne
Messy Church Team Member, Bible Reading Fellowship

What is church?

For most of us who grew up within an established worshipping community, the word 'church' comes with a set of clear descriptors. Church happens in a specially designed building, on a specific day, at certain times and with a service that follows a familiar pattern. It is something that we feel has always happened this way and so it is hard to imagine that church could take any other form.

Hard to imagine it may be, but the truth is that church hasn't always been this way. History tells a different story. Everything changes with time, so it shouldn't be a surprise to learn that church has also adapted itself to speak to each new generation.

The gospel hasn't changed, of course, and people still have big questions about life, death and God and they still look for answers, but how we meet those people with their questions, needs to look different, and perhaps nowhere more so than in the area of sharing our faith with children and young people today.

Fresh Expressions

The term 'fresh expressions of church' was first coined in the document 'Mission Shaped Church' published in 1994. What began as an Anglican initiative in 2004 has now become an ecumenical movement called Fresh Expressions; the Church of Scotland formally entered into partnership with Fresh Expressions in 2013. The challenge was and is to find a new wineskin of church to bring the new wine of the gospel to this current generation.

The Fresh Expressions movement explains that a 'fresh expression is a form of church for our changing culture established primarily for the benefit of people who are not yet members of any church'. All fresh expressions have an emphasis on mission and of being culturally appropriate through listening to the people they want to reach and among whom they wish to form a church.

On the Fresh Expressions website there are many stories of fresh expressions that involve children and young people, including Skateboard Church, Cook Church, and Cell Church, each with its own catchy title such as The Den, Grafted, Sorted, The Ark and Holy Commotion. Those involving children have

usually built on existing models, such as after-school clubs and special weekend events. Some 'praise and play' groups for pre-schoolers come under this same umbrella.

All this has pushed the boundaries of what we understand as church. To the extent that these are outward-looking groups working with those new to faith and helping them to become disciples of Jesus, they are surely being church. Nevertheless questions remain as to whether there needs to be something more. What about their relationship with the standard model of church that meets on a Sunday for example, with its rich traditions and tried and tested understandings of worship as well as wisdom about how Christians best grow in their faith? And how can a church that focuses on only one age or interest group be truly church, if its congregation never encounters other Christians who may not share their particular enthusiasms and who may be of a different generation?

Messy Church

There are some fresh expressions of church that do aim to be truly all-age. Among these, Messy Church, which began life in 2004, stands out.

Sunday morning family services at St Wilfred's near Portsmouth were no longer attracting new people and numbers in the traditional Sunday school were in decline so the congregation considered whether there was a new way and a better time to meet with families. After consultation they decided to begin a new shape of church after school during the week. What was unique, however, was that this would be a meeting for all ages with children accompanied by parents or carers.

The medium for the learning and worship was interactive and creative from the start. Bible stories were explored through

ands-on activities which led to a short celebration followed by a shared meal together. This shape of church caught the imagination of others who heard about it through the Fresh Expressions website, so in the following years many other churches began their own Messy Churches.

There are five key values that sustain the Messy Church formula – hospitality, creativity, celebration, being for all ages and, most importantly, being centred on Christ. Nevertheless, Messy Church has often been misunderstood. It was never intended to be a fresh expression just for children, although many still interpret the 'messy' label to mean that. In fact, the term 'messy' is about all of us, with our messy lives that we need to bring to God and our own often messy journeys of faith.

In the last twenty years there have been new insights that have influenced how churches have worked with children and young people. The traditional model of a separate Sunday school for children's work has, for example, been challenged by research into children's spirituality. Children can be spiritually very mature at any age and are not 'Christians in waiting'. This has led to a re-evaluation of how best to nurture that spirituality and in particular the importance of including other age groups and generations in the mix. Faith nurtured in a multigenerational context has been found to be much more likely to stick.

It is within this framework that Messy Church shares and nurtures faith. Messy Church is as much for the adults as it is for the children; the presence of children simply reminds every one of the way to grow in faith, namely with wonder, openness and in a spirit of discovery like a child. But saying that Messy Church is for all is nevertheless challenging. For example, how do we encourage dads and older children that this is a church for them, if activities tend towards crafts for younger children? And how can we share the gospel within Messy Church without a sermon or a quality period of worship? Is it enough that it is gossiped at the activity tables, explored in the interactive storytelling of the celebration and during the conversations at the meal through one-to-one or family-to-family relationships? And what about discipleship? There are no neat answers to this and in many ways Messy Church is helping the whole church to reconsider what discipleship needs to looks like in the twenty-first century. ■

THINK

How do you feel about labelling age or interest group gatherings that don't meet on a Sunday as church? In what ways do they fulfil or fall short of your idea of what church should be?

Do you know about or have you experienced any fresh expression of church with children and young people in your community? What has inspired you and what has raised questions in your mind?

One of the core values of Messy Church is that it is all-age. What do you feel about nurturing children and young people into faith in a multigenerational setting rather than in age-related groups? What in your view are the advantages and disadvantages of doing this?

READ

Margaret Withers, **Mission-shaped Children: moving towards a child-centred church,** (London: Church House Publishing, 2006)

George Lings (ed.), **Messy Church Theology: exploring the significance of Messy Church for the wider church,** (Abingdon: The Bible Reading Fellowship, 2013)

Ian Paul (ed.), Being Messy, **Being Church: exploring the direction of travel for today's church,** (Abingdon: The Bible Reading Fellowship, 2017)

Paul Moore, **Making disciples in Messy Church: growing faith in an all-age community,** (Abingdon: The Bible Reading Fellowship, 2013)

ACT

Using the Fresh Expressions or Messy Church websites, identify a fresh expression of church with children and young people near you and pay them a visit.

Talk with the leaders at your church about the thinking behind creating a multi-generational congregation and identify some positive ways forward to explore this in your own church.

Have a go at running a one-off pilot Messy Church. Contact your Messy Church Regional Co-ordinator for initial help and ideas **www.messychurch.org.uk/regional-coordinators**

RESOURCE

The Bible Reading Fellowship produce many Messy Church resources such as the Get Messy Magazine, Extreme Crafts for Messy Church, and a guide to Starting your Messy Church

www.messychurch.org.uk

www.freshexpressions.org.uk

SCHOOL CHAPLAINCY

Steve Younger

Minister of High Blantyre Baptist Church and PhD Candidate, University of Glasgow

Scotland's schools have been following the 'Curriculum for Excellence' for a decade now. The focus is not just on curricular excellence and on closing the attainment gap but also on character formation. As well as a new assessment structure, schools actively foster four capacities in every pupil with a view to making them responsible citizens, effective contributors, successful learners and confident individuals. Getting it right for every child is the shared responsibility of every staff member. With this comes a commitment to the health and wellbeing of every pupil. This specifically includes their mental, spiritual and social development.

Religious Observance

The new format of 'Religious Observance' in schools plays a key part in achieving this. Though the title 'Religious Observance' goes back to the Education (Scotland) Act of 1872, it no longer refers to the kind of instruction and enculturation envisaged then. A growing number of local authorities have re-named Religious Observance as 'Time for Reflection'. Whichever title is used, Religious Observance is still a statutory requirement in all Scottish schools in both the primary and secondary sectors.

Religious Observance is currently defined as "community acts which aim to promote the spiritual development of all members of the school community and express and celebrate the shared values of the school community".[36] This is to be done through targeting six 'Sensings':

- Sensing mystery - experiences of awe, wonder and mystery about the natural world, human achievement and for some a divinity

- Sensing values - attitudes and feelings about what is really important, what really matters

- Sensing meaningfulness - the ability to make connections or to see potential patterns in one's life that give it meaning

- Sensing a changed quality in awareness - the feeling of being 'at one' with nature, oneself and others

- Sensing otherness - the sentiment that humans are more than their physical elements

- Sensing challenge - being challenged and moved by experiences such as love, beauty, goodness, joy, com-passion, injustice, evil, suffering, death

In 2011 the Scottish Government issued guidance to all head teachers stating that in recognition of Scotland's Christian heritage, non-denominational schools are "encouraged to draw upon the rich resources of this tradition when planning religious observance. However, many school communities encompass pupils and staff from faiths other than Christianity or with no faith commitment, and this must be taken fully into account in supporting spiritual development. It is of central importance that all pupils and staff can participate with integrity in forms of religious observance without compromise to their personal faith".[37] For most schools this means a commitment to regular, specific Religious Observance events at the very least.

The role of churches

Many schools are realising that this kind of capacity building and sensing is beyond their expertise. Chaplains and churches are seen as ideal partners in delivering quality Religious Observance. As fewer and fewer children come through the doors of their local churches this open door to partner with schools becomes ever more important and strategic. John Caperon's comment on schools in England rings true for those of us in Scotland as well: "the church's most significant work among and for the young is no longer carried out in Sunday schools and through church youth work in the context of the parish, as was the case in the 19th and 20th centuries, but by chaplains and supporting Christian staff in the context of …. School".[38]

More than assemblies

School chaplaincy is not and has never been a parish 'right'; chaplains and churches can only partner with a local school at the invitation of the Head Teacher. Religious Observance is the responsibility of schools, not of churches'. Yet the partnership of church and school through chaplaincy is about far more than the minister or the youth worker parachuting in for regular assemblies. With time, knowledge, training and commitment will come multiple opportunities. chaplaincy is a form of incarnational ministry and is a growth area across all kinds of schools. Chaplains are not visitors, they are part of the community, they work with people, eat with them, and queue for coffee with them.[39]

At a conference of school chaplains in South Lanarkshire (April 2015), these were just some of the activities in which chaplains listed their involvement. It will hopefully give you some ideas! ■

- participating in school trips
- having a pastoral supporting role during times of extreme difficulty or crisis for school communities
- supporting school community events
- providing pastoral care and support for staff, pupils and their families where appropriate
- assisting a school to support and develop their Religious Observance calendar of events
- leading or helping pupil groups with a particular religious, moral or citizenship interest
- providing links between school and local community groups
- contributing to extra-curricular clubs in consultation and agreement with the Head Teacher
- Scripture Union groups
- visiting classes at the invitation of staff to complement the curriculum
- visiting places of worship
- and any other activity agreed between the Head Teacher and the chaplain

36. *Report of the Religious Observance Review Group*, Scottish Executive, 2004

37. https://education.gov.scot/

38. John Caperon, *A Vital Ministry: Chaplaincy in Schools in the Post-Christian Era*, (SCM Press, 2015), p.133

39. Anthony Buckley, *Help, There's a School in my Parish: ED16*, (Grove Books Ltd, 2013), p.22

THINK

In twenty-first century Scotland the school is increasingly the primary context for the moral, social, physical and spiritual development of children. What are the implications of this for your congregation?

Which Biblical word or role would best describe your vision for engaging with your local schools, for example 'ambassador', 'apostle', 'evangelist', 'prophet', 'servant' or something else?

READ

Anthony Buckley, **Help, There's a School in my Parish: ED16,** (Grove Books Ltd, 2013)

John Caperon, **A Vital Ministry: Chaplaincy in Schools in the Post-Christian Era,** (SCM Press, 2015)

Ronni Lamont, **Understanding Children Understanding God,** (SPCK, 2007)

Diane Tregale, **Fresh Expressions of School Chaplaincy: ED6,** (Grove Books Ltd, 2011)

M. Withers, **Local Church, Local School: Practical and Creative Ways for Churches to Serve Local Primary Schools,** (Bible Reading Fellowship, 2010)

ACT

Encourage your congregation to create a single paragraph vision for working in partnership with your local schools.

Find out who in your congregation is involved in your local school(s) in some way and consider how that involvement can be co-ordinated and developed. Consider instigating a chaplaincy team where there currently isn't one.

RESOURCE

'Bubblegum 'n' Fluff' and '(Easter Code)' - programmes for Church and school partnerships to present the Christmas and Easter stories www.calderside.org.uk

Christian Values in Education www.cve-scotland.org.uk

Scripture Union Scotland www.suscotland.org.uk

Serve Your Local School www.syls.org.uk

Prayer Spaces in Schools www.prayerspacesinschools.com

My Story

Alison Kennedy

Youth and Community Worker, Flemmington Hallside Parish Church

At the age of twenty-four, with very little background knowledge of Christian faith, and at a crisis point in my life, a family member invited me to meet with his minister. Soon after this, that minister invited me to visit Church (yes, it was a very scary prospect, as I knew I was just not the type of person to fit in).

I managed to stick it out for a few months, although it wasn't a comfortable experience for me - these people were so very different, and so knowledgeable, and so very 'churchy', and God knew what he was doing when he invited them to be part of his church.

However, getting up on a Sunday morning and going to church gave me a purpose for that day, so I persevered. After a few months I received another invitation, to help lead at the church's youth group on a Sunday evening. Me? Me who knew very little of the wonders of God's word, surely I wasn't worthy of this invitation...

In between all of this happening came my biggest invitation of all, the invitation from God himself to come and follow Him. Totally unworthy, but totally loved!

When I reflect on my story, what I see as a recurrent theme is invitation, specifically an invitation to belong. Now that I am employed as a youth worker, invitation and belonging are always in my mind when I think about the work we do with our young people. At the beginning of Jesus ministry, he begins with an invitation, 'come, follow me', so it seems vital to start there with our children and young people.

So, how do we go about giving them an invitation they will want to accept? Although church can be a good place for us to invite our young people to, Sunday mornings are not always easy for them, with sports schedules, family visits and lie-ins after a busy week.

One way we do this in our congregation is by our youth leaders hosting a gathering of the older young people in our homes on a weekday evening. It is through personal invitation so they know they are valued when they receive that invitation. Together we create a community that's all about relationship and sharing life; we share some food, we talk, we laugh, we cry. They get to hear our family bickering and see what is normal for us going on around them, warts and all, the dirty dishes, the forgotten dusting. It's all about being open and available to one another.

Understanding that many young people can find meaning in groups, gangs, being part of the crowd, this environment allows them be part of a group, in a safe and nurturing place that can open up avenues where they can share their hopes, their fears, and their lives. Within that secure place there is the time to grow in relationship and in faith; tricky questions are asked, and we ponder these together.

The true invitation from God may well come in a place like these small communities, and with that invitation comes a sense of freedom, full acceptance and belonging. Our young people may also make their own invitation there, asking Jesus into their lives. Jesus was once invited to a wedding in Cana, without that invitation, that first miracle may not have happened. The invitation to all of us is to invite Jesus into every area of our lives, listening for his further invitations and seeking his guidance in all we do. ∎

My Story

Debbie Johnstone

Volunteer at Hot Chocolate, Dundee

Do you know that feeling when you have had a taste of something that's exciting, slightly scary, but awesome, and you know that you so want be part of it? If you do, then let me introduce you to Hot Chocolate. If you don't then here is a taster: privilege, respect, other world, developing, trust, listening ear, chance to question, a safe place, to be able to speak without being judged, confidential, honest, opportunity to explore, affirming, if I change my opinion - that's OK, chance to educate, perspective, included.

Hot Chocolate is an organisation with a Christian foundation. Since 2001 many young people have been served, helped and shown God's love. Each week young people drop in to take part in activities they have identified, such as music, art, film, and interest based group activities.[40]

Volunteering at Hot Chocolate gave me the privilege to share some space and time with young people who are establishing trust and respect in a safe place where they know they will not be judged. Some young people live in turmoil, where adults in their world are not always reliable, trustworthy or affirming. Hot Chocolate provides an 'other world' where the adults they meet are listening and providing opportunities to explore issues with alternative perspectives, exploring risk-taking behaviours and their possible consequences.

I once heard Hot Chocolate being described as a safe place for vulnerable young people, however, I was the one who felt vulnerable when volunteering for the first time. One year on, I still feel vulnerable. One thing that has changed is my perspective on vulnerability. Previously, I viewed vulnerability only as a weakness to be avoided, however, now I also see vulnerability as a strength. Brene Brown expertly explains the concept of managing vulnerability to build resilience in her book 'Daring Greatly'.[41] It is amazing to see Hot Chocolate young people grow in resilience as they build relationships, face fears, make mistakes and have another go. An opportunity to volunteer on Youth Team is given to those young people who want and are ready to develop further. This is so exciting; it's a bit like watching plants grow from seedlings to fully fledged flowers, some needing a bit more attention to than others.

On reflection, in my congregation I have led our youth ministry for around twelve years, organising residential weekends and a youth exchange trip with the Scots Kirk in Rotterdam and planning programmes for teaching, training and recruiting volunteers. All of these were controlled by adults for young people. The significant difference between that and the work at Hot Chocolate is that one is orchestrated and the other organic. I now know which I prefer. ■

40. Hot Chocolate, Induction Pack Week#2. *HC and me!* Hot Chocolate Trust
41. Brene Brown, *Daring Greatly: how the courage to be vulnerable transforms the way we live, love, parent and lead*, (Penguin Life, 2015)

WHAT DOES BEING PART OF THE CHURCH MEAN TO YOU?

Feeling safe
Callum, 10

Have friends
Sophie, 8

It's awesome!
I get to find out
more about who
God is!
Kirstin, 15

Being part of a kind
and supportive
church.
A great opportunity
to praise God
through worship
Edmund, 15

It means I get
to see friends and
do fun activities
Daniel, 11

Running and
seeing friends
Anna, 4

To learn
about God
Ryan, 7

Belonging to a welcoming
congregation and feeling
part of a church that
offers guidance and
support
Nadine, 24

Part of who I am.
Learning
about God
Sarah, 10

I am loved
Luke, 15

WHAT DO YOU NEED FROM THE CHURCH OF SCOTLAND?

The word of God
Iain, 11

Bibles that are easier to understand
Alistair, 8

Hot chocolate and chat
Nathan, 15

More running about
Alistair, 4

To learn
Samantha, 6

To be able to enjoy church
Daniel, 11

Happiness and playing with friends and more about God
Charlotte, 7

I need it to be there in the future. More arts and crafts
Sarah, 10

To know all young people in the Church of Scotland have a passion for Christ and want to commit to their faith
Kirstin, 15

We would like there to be more events for our age group
Megan, 13

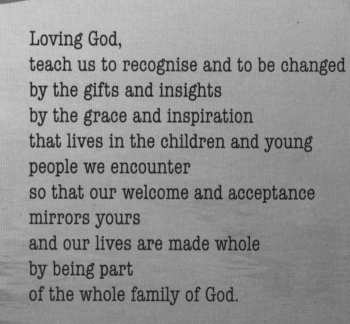

Loving God,
teach us to recognise and to be changed
by the gifts and insights
by the grace and inspiration
that lives in the children and young
people we encounter
so that our welcome and acceptance
mirrors yours
and our lives are made whole
by being part
of the whole family of God.

Liz Crumlish
Path of Renewal Co-ordinator, Ministries Council